COLLEGE COOKING

COLLEGE

COOKING

FEED YOURSELF AND YOUR FRIENDS

• • •

MEGAN & JILL CARLE

TEN SPEED PRESS
Berkeley | Toronto

Ten Speed Press
PO Box 7123
Berkeley, California 94707
www.tenspeed.com

Distributed in Australia by Simon and Schuster Australia, in Canada by Ten Speed Press Canada, in New Zealand by Southern Publishers Group, in South Africa by Real Books, and in the United Kingdom and Europe by Publishers Group UK.

Cover and text design by Betsy Stromberg

Library of Congress Cataloging-in-Publication Data
Carle, Megan.
  College cooking : feed yourself and your friends / by Megan and Jill Carle.
     p. cm.
  Includes index.
  ISBN-13: 978-1-58008-826-8
  ISBN-10: 1-58008-826-0
  1. Cookery. I. Carle, Jill. II. Title.
  TX652.C3277 2007
  641.5—dc22
                              2006030526

Printed in China

3 4 5 6 7 8 9 10 — 11 10 09 08 07

CONTENTS

ACKNOWLEDGMENTS

As always, there are people that deserve our undying gratitude for their continued help and support.

To Lorena Jones, Lily Binns, and Brie Mazurek of Ten Speed Press: Thanks for believing in a couple of kids and keeping us on track, which is no small feat.

To Jessica Boone: It's amazing that you're able to take fabulous photos even with us singing every musical known to man at the top of our lungs. That's talent.

To Yvonne Govea: You set a new standard in friendship. You showed up to help every day, knowing you were going to be subjected to the dreaded musicals. We promise we will never again play *The Sound of Music* when you are around.

To our ace team of taste testers, Jim Govea, Chris and Diane Worsley, Amy, Todd and Connor Tennison, Mark and April Barry, and Richard Rhoades: You guys showed up every day for weeks on end to be our guinea pigs. Your honest comments and critiques helped us fine-tune these recipes. This book is better because of all of you.

To Mom and Dad, last on the list, but first in our hearts: Thanks for always supporting us and not complaining too much when we stuck you with all of the dishes. We'd like to tell you we promise never to do that again, but we probably will.

—Megan and Jill
M & J

INTRODUCTION

I learned the hard way that cooking in your first apartment is not the same as cooking at Mom's house. When I left for college, I had grandiose ideas of the meals I would prepare. After all, I could cook and had written two cookbooks to prove it. This would be a piece of cake. I was moving into a furnished two-bedroom dorm apartment with a kitchen, a living room, and, oh yeah, three roommates I had never met. I was loaded down with all the food staples necessary to amaze my new friends with my culinary skills. Well . . . it didn't quite work out that way. I just wanted to make chocolate chip cookies, something I had done at least a hundred times before, but I got stymied on the first step: put the butter in a bowl. After looking through all four cabinets in the world's smallest kitchen, I soon realized that the university's idea of "furnished" did not include mixing bowls. But hey, I'm adaptable, so I put the butter in the banged-up stockpot with the peeling nonstick coating. Next came mixing in the sugar—oops, no mixer. It kind of went downhill from there. The final straw was realizing there were no baking sheets. Not that it mattered because the oven was too small to fit a normal baking sheet anyway. I ended up baking the cookies six at a time in a 9 by 13-inch pan.

Despite all the problems, my new roommates loved the cookies and were thrilled that I could cook. (None of them had progressed past ramen noodles and frozen dinners.) After a trip to the local discount store to supplement the not-so-furnished kitchen, I was good to go. I began cooking meals every night for the four of us, and I soon learned that an ancillary benefit to cooking was getting to meet a lot of people. I'm not sure if it was word of mouth or the food aromas wafting through the air, but other people in my dorm seemed to stop by to visit whenever I was cooking. It didn't take long before friends were offering to buy ingredients if I would turn them into "real food." As hard as it may be for our parents to believe, even college students get sick of fast food.

After watching so many of our friends stumble around the kitchen, Jill and I decided that we needed to write a book specifically geared for college students. In other words, very little equipment, very little cooking experience, and very little money. (We are particularly well versed in very little money.) The recipes included in this book are dishes we adapted to fit our college lifestyle in different ways. Some of them are things that we make just because the leftovers taste so good and they'll make meals for several days. Some are low in calories to help balance out those overindulged days. Some go easy on the budget, and others are like real home-cooked meals.

We also had to make some changes to the ingredients. The first time you have to walk home from the grocery store and trudge up several flights of stairs with all your food, you'll understand. Food is heavy. Some things we couldn't do anything about, but things on our list like chicken stock soon became dried chicken bouillon. One container of dried bouillon weighs a few ounces, but the equivalent amount of chicken stock weighs over twelve pounds. (Okay, so the fact that dried bouillon also costs about one-tenth what stock does might also have something to do with it.) We also started using seasoning blends so we wouldn't have to buy so many different spices. The point is, you might find that some of the ingredients in these recipes are different from what you'd expect, but we've chosen everything for a reason and the finished dishes still taste great.

We've included lots of helpful information to make the transition to your own kitchen a little smoother. There are lists of equipment and basic food items along with a short cooking class to help you avoid some common mistakes. There are tips throughout the book to help you save a little money, adjust recipes for vegetarians, and cut out unnecessary calories. And we couldn't resist adding a smattering of trivia just for fun.

If you've never cooked before, start with the "Survival Cooking" recipes and work your way up from there. In no time at all, you'll be able to handle the "Impressing Your Date" recipes. If you have messed around in the kitchen before, just dive in, there're lots of terrific dishes to choose from.

—Megan

KITCHEN BASICS

Here are some basics about ingredients and cooking that you should know before starting in on the recipes. We don't explain this stuff throughout the book because it would be incredibly redundant and take up a lot of space, so you'll probably want to refer back here often.

INGREDIENTS

Bouillon: We use dried bouillon instead of canned stock because it's cheaper and a lot lighter to carry home from the store. We buy the granules because it dissolves faster, but the cubes are fine too. Each cube is equivalent to 1 teaspoon of the granules. Just make sure you cook the cubes enough for them to completely dissolve.

Butter: We've always used salted. It used to be because that's what Mom bought, but now it's because we prefer salted butter to use on bread and it's too much of a hassle to buy salted and unsalted butter.

Cooking spray: We say butter or spray the pan in the recipes. We always spray. It's faster, you don't have to get your hands all greasy, and it's fat-free. We use plain, unflavored cooking spray and since we are paying for it now, we buy the store brand. It's cheaper and works just as well as the name brands.

Cornstarch: This is a fast and easy way to thicken sauces, but it can cause a real mess if it's not used properly. It must be mixed with a little bit of cold liquid before being added to the sauce or it will immediately form large lumps that will never smooth out. You don't need a lot of liquid, just enough to form a smooth, pourable mixture. One other tip about cornstarch; it doesn't have much staying power. It's meant to be used right before serving. If it cooks for more than 10 minutes your sauce will begin to thin out again.

Eggs: All the eggs in the recipes are large. All other ingredients are medium unless we mention a size. In other words, if we just say potato, we mean a medium-size potato. If we say large potato, we mean a large potato. Just don't get carried away. If it's big enough to make you say, "Wow, look at that!" it's too big.

Fruits and vegetables: Wash all of the fruits and vegetables before you use them. Dirt and other people's germs should never be ingredients in any recipe.

Herbs: We use dried herbs more often in our recipes than fresh herbs simply because they are cheaper and easier to have on hand. When we use fresh herbs it's because the dish needs the slightly different flavor that the fresh herb provides. Dried herbs are more potent than their fresh counterparts. That said, now we'll tell you that it's not always true. Dried herbs are more potent than fresh for the first three months. Once that time has passed they begin to lose their potency and after six months, their flavoring power drops drastically. Manufacturers recommend replacing dried herbs every six months. Since that is not feasible on our budget, we simply taste each dish and add more if it seems like the herb has lost some of its punch.

Lemon juice: Freshly squeezed lemon juice has a fresher flavor than the bottled version, but we still always keep a bottle of lemon juice in the refrigerator. If we are planning ahead, we will buy fresh lemons. But the reality is that the closest grocery store to us is about a mile away, and if we don't have fresh ones on hand, we aren't likely to walk there just to get them.

Mayonnaise and sour cream: Generally, we use low-fat because we're all for saving a few calories when you can't taste a difference. Just keep in mind that the low-fat versions have a tendency to get watery after they are mixed with other ingredients. So, if you are making chicken salad to eat right away, the low-fat mayo is fine, but if you want to serve it later, either use regular mayo or mix in the low-fat version right before serving. And we say mayonnaise in the recipes, but we actually use Miracle Whip. That's what Mom always bought, and it's what we are used to. Use whichever one you prefer; it doesn't matter.

Potatoes: There are many different types of potatoes available in stores, but we usually use red or russets (also called Idaho). Red potatoes are more expensive than russets, but they are also less starchy. Since they hold their shape better when sliced, we always use them for potato salads. For almost everything else we use russet potatoes. They are inexpensive and work well for baking, mashing, or frying.

Puff pastry and phyllo dough: We are huge fans of frozen, which is easy to use and makes you look like a pro. In most grocery stores you will find them in the freezer section by the desserts. Just make sure to thaw them in the refrigerator or the condensation will make the dough sticky and hard to work with.

Rice: With long grain, short grain, medium grain, white, and brown, the variety of different types of rice can be overwhelming. The good news is any of those will work in these recipes. The difference between long, medium and short grain rice is in the starch that is released during cooking. Short grain rice releases a lot of starch and is sticky when cooked. Long grain rice releases much less starch and is fluffy when cooked. Medium grain falls right in the middle. White and brown rice start out the same, but white rice has the nutritious, high fiber bran coating removed. Because brown rice still has the bran coating it takes 10 to 15 minutes longer to cook than white rice. Armed with all that information, you can choose whichever type you like. But, truth be told, we buy whichever one is cheapest.

TECHNIQUES

Cooking asparagus: To avoid the woody portion the ends of asparagus should be broken off, not cut. Hold the stem end in one hand and about 2 inches below the tip in the other. Bend the asparagus and break off the end. It may seem that you are discarding more than you should, but what you are throwing away is the tough portion that isn't pleasant to eat. Cook asparagus in the same manner as broccoli, checking it often. It should be soft, but not mushy.

Cooking broccoli: Broccoli is another vegetable that seems to cause people trouble. This one's easy, don't overcook it. Place the broccoli in a pan with about 1 inch of water. Bring the water to a boil, cover, and cook over medium-high heat for 4 minutes. Check for tenderness and cook for 1 to 2 more minutes if necessary. Broccoli should be bright green and tender, but not soggy. Under no circumstances should broccoli ever be cooked for more than 7 minutes. After 7 minutes it loses its color and becomes soggy.

Cooking pasta: The key to making perfect pasta is a lot of boiling water. If you don't have enough water or the water isn't boiling when you put in the pasta, you will end up with a large gelatinous mass. To cook one pound of pasta, use at least a 3-quart saucepan. Fill the pan to about 1 inch from the top with water, add a teaspoon of salt, and bring the water to a full boil. Add the pasta and stir frequently as it cooks. The cooking time will depend on the thickness of pasta; angel hair will take about 5 minutes, but linguine or penne could take up to 15 minutes. Pasta is usually cooked al dente, which literally translates as "to the tooth," meaning it should offer slight resistance when bitten into, but not be soft. The easiest way to test for doneness is to remove one piece with a fork and taste it. Since Mom's not around you could always try the throw it against the wall and see if it sticks method. Just remember, she's also not around to clean it up.

Frying with oil: There are whole books written about kitchen safety, but the issue we feel compelled to mention here is, oil and water don't mix. Whenever you are frying something in oil make sure to use a pan that is at least twice the depth of the oil. This allows room for the oil to bubble up without running over the sides of the pan. Also, make sure that the food you are adding to the oil is as dry as possible. We know that it is impossible for everything you fry to be completely dry, but it's not hard to avoid excess liquids. In the unlikely event that you do cause a grease fire, DO NOT use water to put it out. Water will cause the oil to spatter, spreading the fire. Sprinkling baking soda on the fire will put it right out.

Peeling garlic: Smash the garlic clove by placing it on a flat surface, laying the blade of a large knife flat on top of the garlic, and hitting the knife with the heel of your hand. Remove and discard the papery skin and finely chop the garlic.

Separating eggs: To separate egg yolks from egg whites, crack the egg and hold it upright over a small bowl. Remove the top part of the shell, trapping the egg yolk and allowing the white to drip into the bowl. Then transfer the yolk into the empty half of the shell allowing the remainder of the white to fall into the bowl. If this method seems too confusing, crack the whole egg into a small bowl and gently lift out the egg yolk, allowing the white to run out between your fingers. There is one hard and fast rule for separating eggs. When you are separating multiple eggs, always, always, always separate them over a small bowl first. Once each egg is separated they can be added to the larger bowl. If you break a yolk into the small bowl you throw away one egg. If you break it into the large bowl you have to through away all the eggs and start over.

TOOLS AND EQUIPMENT

If you read the introduction, you know that I learned rather quickly what items I needed to actually be able to cook a meal. (If you didn't read the intro, you just have to trust me.) The following is a list of the basic items that you should have in order to cook the dishes in this or most other cookbooks. (Not, of course, that you would dream of using any other cookbook.)

The first section is required items and the second section includes things that aren't necessary, but certainly are helpful. It may seem like a lot of stuff, but we aren't talking about top-of-the-line brands here. If you head to the local discount or thrift store, you should be able to get all of these items for around $100.

You don't need to buy everything at once. You can get the basics and fill in the rest as you go along. Better yet, you can give the list to your mom as your holiday or birthday list. If your mom is anything like ours, you will end up with most of the items on the list and they will be better quality than you would buy yourself.

NECESSARY ITEMS

Set of pots and pans: These usually come in eight-piece sets that include a 1-quart covered saucepan, a 2-quart covered saucepan, a 5-quart covered Dutch oven (stockpot), and 2 sauté pans. They vary greatly in price, running from as low as $15 into the hundreds.

While your immediate reaction may be to go for the $15 set, they aren't much stronger than aluminum foil and will not last too long before the handles fall off. The sets that are around $50 are decent and will last for a few years.

Knives: Take it from someone who knows, owning one steak knife gets old rather quickly. It would be ideal to have one of those six- or eight-piece sets, but what you truly need is a paring knife, a large knife for chopping, and, if you can afford it, a serrated knife for cutting bread.

Baking pans: You will need to have one baking sheet (usually 11 by 15 inches, but make sure it will fit in your oven), one 9 by 13-inch pan, and one 8-inch square pan. If it fits in your budget, it's helpful to have two 9 by 13-inch pans and two baking sheets.

Blender: This is the only electric appliance we use in the book (except for a microwave, which isn't required), and you could probably live without it, but it is extremely helpful to have one. It doesn't need to be the mega model; the one I have was on sale at the grocery store for $13 and it works fine.

Stacking bowls: These are graduated bowls that come in plastic, glass, or metal. Get either the glass or plastic because they can go in the microwave. At home we have glass, but I bought a set of four plastic bowls at a discount store for $4, and they are fine.

Colander: Plastic or metal doesn't matter, just get one large enough to hold a pound of cooked pasta.

Can opener: Electric is nice, but handheld works fine too.

Spatulas: If you have nonstick pans you will need a plastic spatula, but the metal ones are thinner and often work better for taking cookies off baking sheets and getting food out of baking pans intact. Buy one of each if you can afford it.

Measuring cups: A set of stacking dry measuring cups and a 2-cup liquid measuring cup would be best. (Contrary to popular belief, a dry cup measures slightly less than a liquid cup.) But, if you absolutely can't afford both, get the stacking set.

Measuring spoons: Trust me on this one, buy a set with the measurements pressed into the metal or plastic. If the numbers are just printed on they'll wash off after a while and it gets quite confusing to try to figure out which one is which.

HELPFUL ITEMS

Large spoons: Either metal or wooden. These will save you a ton of time you'd otherwise spend fishing out little spoons when they slide into a pan full of food.

Rubber scraper: Scrapers are helpful indeed if you plan to do any baking. I like the ones made of soft rubber rather than hard plastic because they bend, making it easier to scrape everything out of a bowl.

Cutting board: Cutting on the counter will dull your knives and tick off your apartment manager. It doesn't matter if it is wood or plastic, both work.

Grater: This can save you a lot of time. I like the box graters with three different grating sides and one slicing side.

Garlic press: If you hate the smell of garlic on your hands, this is a must-have. You can certainly chop garlic with a knife, but the press is faster and you can press the garlic right into the pan.

Hot pads or oven mits: These come in very handy. You can use a kitchen towel instead of hot pads, but remember, water conducts heat. If the towel is the least bit damp, you will feel the heat immediately.

Pastry brushes: Again, these are not necessary, but they do come in handy. I bought a set of three for $1 at a dollar store.

Vegetable peeler: You can peel fruit and vegetables with a knife, but I say, why bother. As cheap as vegetable peelers are, it seems silly to hassle with a knife.

STOCKING YOUR PANTRY

There is nothing more frustrating than deciding to cook something and then realizing you don't have all of the ingredients. This list won't stop that from happening, but it will help. (Besides, you can save a lot of money if you can get Mom and Dad to buy some of these before you leave for school.)

The first section lists the basic items that you'll use all the time. The second section contains more specific items that you may or may not need, depending on your tastes. The third section is the essentials for making desserts. Personally, we think these belong with the items you use all the time, but you can decide for yourself.

WHAT EVERY KITCHEN SHOULD HAVE

Cooking spray	Mexican seasoning
Salt	Italian seasoning
Pepper	Ground ginger
Flour	Fresh garlic
Sugar	Butter or margarine
Cornstarch	Eggs
Canola oil	Milk
Soy sauce	Pasta
Lemon juice	Rice
Dried chicken bouillon	Potatoes
Dried beef bouillon	Onions
White wine vinegar	

OTHER THINGS TO THINK ABOUT

Parmesan cheese	Chili powder
Crushed red pepper	Chili paste
Olive oil	Cajun seasoning
Curry powder	Nutmeg

BAKING ESSENTIALS

Baking soda	Cinnamon
Baking powder	Vanilla
Brown sugar	Chocolate chips
Confectioners' sugar	

SURVIVAL COOKING

If you can open a can, use a knife, and boil water, you can handle these recipes. These are some of our favorite dinners, but they're all **incredibly easy to make**. As an added bonus, most of them make a lot and are good reheated so you won't have to cook every night. If you've never cooked anything before, start with the Chicken with Rice. All you have to do is open a can. Once you've made that, you will realize that if you can read, you can make these recipes. We've made the directions as simple as possible and tried to give you visual cues of what things should look like as you go along. We promise there are no fancy tricks here. Just follow the directions step by step, and you can't go wrong.

CHICKEN WITH RICE

J: This is a perfect dish in my book. It's super simple to put together, it makes a lot, and it tastes terrific even when it's reheated. When my mom makes this, she cuts up a whole chicken. But I'm only willing to go so far to save money and cutting up whole chickens is beyond that point. I buy whatever parts of the chicken are on sale and already cut up.

SERVES 4 TO 6

1 (10-ounce) can cream of mushroom soup

1 (1.3-ounce) package dry onion soup mix

1 cup white rice

1¼ cups water

3 to 4 pounds bone-in chicken pieces

Preheat the oven to 350°F.

Stir together the cream of mushroom soup, onion soup mix, and rice in a 9 by 13-inch baking pan. Add the water and stir until fairly smooth. (The water will not get mixed in completely, just make sure the rice is evenly distributed in the pan.) Place the chicken pieces on top of the rice mixture and cover the pan with aluminum foil. Bake for 30 minutes. Carefully remove the foil and bake for another 30 minutes, or until the chicken is lightly browned. (You can also make this with boneless chicken: just leave the foil on for 45 minutes and take it off for the last 15 minutes.) Remove from the oven and serve immediately.

 FOOD FOR THOUGHT

Rice is a complex carbohydrate, which means that it contains starch and fiber. Complex carbohydrates are digested slowly, allowing the body to utilize the energy released over a longer period, which is nutritionally efficient. It has a low sodium content and contains potassium, which helps maintain your fluid and electrolyte balance, and the B vitamins that break down carbohydrates, fats, and proteins and are essential for your skin, hair, eyes, and liver.

TUNA NOODLE CASSEROLE

J: This is how I like tuna casserole, but feel free to make it how you like it. With peas, without peas, with cracker crumbs or crushed potato chips on top, it doesn't matter, it's still good. You can also save a few calories by making it with low-fat cream of mushroom soup and you won't even notice the difference.

SERVES 4

12 ounces uncooked noodles

1 (6-ounce) can tuna

1 (10-ounce) can cream of mushroom soup

1 cup frozen peas (optional)

1 teaspoon salt

1/2 teaspoon pepper

Preheat the oven to 350°F. Coat a 2-quart casserole or 9 by 13-inch baking pan with cooking spray or oil.

Bring a large saucepan of salted water to a boil and add the noodles. Cook over medium-high heat, stirring occasionally, for 10 minutes, or until the noodles are al dente. Drain the noodles in a colander.

Meanwhile, drain the tuna and place it in the casserole or baking dish. Add the cream of mushroom soup, peas, salt, and pepper and stir until combined. Add the noodles and stir until they are completely coated with the soup mixture. Bake for 30 minutes, or until lightly browned. Remove from the oven and serve immediately.

VEG OUT

This is also really good as a mushroom casserole. Just leave out the tuna and add 1/2 pound of sautéed sliced mushrooms. Or, if you're really feeling lazy, add a can of drained mushrooms.

FOOD TRIVIA

Casseroles became popular in the 1930s when the Great Depression forced cooks to seek economical solutions for family meals. Tuna casserole became popular during that time when the Campbell's Soup Company was promoting its Cream of Mushroom Soup as a quick and economical way to make a meal. Americans loved the idea of cheap and easy. Nice to know some things never change.

CHICKEN TETRAZZINI

M: Real chicken Tetrazzini combines pasta and chicken in a sauce made with sherry and Parmesan cheese. It should come as no surprise that I have opted for an easier version that uses canned soup and can be made very quickly. Even though it serves four, I sometimes make it just for myself because it's super tasty and makes great leftovers.

SERVES 4 TO 6

1 pound boneless, skinless chicken

1 pound uncooked spaghetti

1 (10-ounce) can cream of chicken soup

1/2 cup grated Parmesan cheese

1 (8-ounce) can sliced mushrooms

1/2 cup milk

1 teaspoon salt

1/2 teaspoon pepper

Preheat the oven to 350°F. Coat a 9 by 13-inch baking pan with cooking spray or oil.

Cut the chicken into 2-inch chunks and place in a small saucepan. Cover with water and cook over medium heat for 15 minutes, or until the chicken is cooked through. (Cut into one of the pieces to make sure there is no pink inside.) Remove from the heat and drain off the water.

Bring a large saucepan of salted water to a boil and add the spaghetti. Cook over medium-high heat, stirring occasionally, for 10 minutes, or until al dente. Drain the spaghetti in a colander.

Meanwhile, cut the cooked chicken into bite-size pieces and place in the baking pan. Add the cream of chicken soup, Parmesan cheese, mushrooms with the juice, milk, salt, and pepper and stir well. Add the spaghetti and toss until it is completely coated and the chicken and mushrooms are fairly evenly distributed. Bake, uncovered, for 30 minutes, or until lightly browned. (If you are in a hurry, you can drain the spaghetti, mix the remaining ingredients in the saucepan, add the spaghetti, and cook over medium heat, stirring constantly, for 5 minutes, or until warmed through.) Remove from the oven and serve immediately.

🥕 VEG OUT

It couldn't be simpler to turn this into a vegetarian dish: leave out the chicken and use cream of mushroom or cream of celery soup. I often add cooked broccoli or spinach, but it's good without them too.

💡 FOOD FOR THOUGHT

With the rise of low-carb diets, pasta seems to be getting a bad rap. But, consider this: one cup of cooked pasta has less than 200 calories; is cholesterol-free, low in fat and sodium, and a good source of thiamin, iron, riboflavin, niacin, and folic acid; and provides 2 grams of dietary fiber and 7 grams of protein. Besides, it's cheap and I like it.

BAKED PENNE PASTA WITH ITALIAN SAUSAGE

M: When I first started college, I was a total pastaholic, not only because it's cheap and you just have to boil water, but because it's so darn good. This is one of my favorite versions. With pasta, Italian sausage, and melted mozzarella, who wouldn't love it. This dish makes a lot, but that's okay because it's also excellent reheated.

SERVES 4 TO 6

1 pound uncooked
penne pasta

1 small onion

2 cloves garlic

1 pound Italian sausage

2 (15-ounce) cans
tomato sauce

2 teaspoons Italian
seasoning

2 cups shredded mozzarella
cheese

BARGAIN SHOPPER

The first time I bought Italian sausage I couldn't believe it was over $5 a pound. When I mentioned it to my mom, she said make your own. After I finished laughing I asked how. It's easy and costs a lot less. Put 1 pound of ground pork, 1 tablespoon finely chopped red pepper, 1 teaspoon finely chopped garlic, 1 tablespoon fennel seed, 1/4 teaspoon crushed red pepper flakes, and 1 teaspoon of black pepper in a bowl and mix it up. That's it.

Preheat the oven to 350°F. Lightly coat a 9 by 13-inch baking pan with oil or cooking spray.

Bring a large saucepan of salted water to a boil and add the pasta. Cook over medium-high heat, stirring occasionally, for 10 minutes, or until al dente. Drain the pasta in a colander.

Meanwhile, peel the onion and chop it into 1/4- to 1/2-inch pieces. Peel the garlic and finely chop. Place the sausage in a sauté pan and add the onion and garlic. (If you have sausage links, cut them into 1/2-inch-thick slices.) Cook over medium-high heat, stirring frequently, for 15 minutes, or until the sausage is completely browned. Drain the grease from the pan, add the tomato sauce and Italian seasoning, and stir until combined.

Spread half of the pasta into the baking pan and top with half of the sauce and 1/3 of the cheese. Layer the remaining pasta, sauce, and cheese and bake for 20 to 25 minutes, until the cheese just begins to brown. Remove from the oven and serve immediately.

TORTILLA SOUP

J: I adore tortilla soup, but a lot of restaurants make it too spicy for me. **SERVES 4**
I'd rather make it at home where I can control the heat by using milder
salsa. This is an easy version that can be made from start to finish in
less than 30 minutes.

6 corn tortillas

2 teaspoons canola oil

Salt

1/2 pound boneless, skinless
chicken breasts

2 tablespoons dried chicken
bouillon

5 cups water

1 cup salsa

1 (14-ounce) can corn kernels

Pepper

1 cup shredded cheddar or
Jack cheese (optional)

Preheat the oven to 400°F.

Cut 2 of the tortillas into thin strips and place on a baking
sheet. Toss the strips in 1 teaspoon of the oil and season with
salt. Bake for 7 to 10 minutes, until crisp.

Chop the remaining 4 tortillas into small (1/4- to 1/2-inch)
pieces.

Cut the chicken into bite-size pieces and place in a large
saucepan with the remaining 1 teaspoon of oil. Cook over
medium-high heat, stirring occasionally, for 5 minutes. Add
the chopped tortillas, bouillon, water, and salsa. Drain the
corn and stir it into the pan. Bring the soup to a boil. Reduce
the heat to medium-low, season with salt and pepper, and
simmer for 15 minutes.

Ladle the soup into bowls and top with the cheese and
crisp tortilla strips.

 FOOD FOR THOUGHT

Using cooking spray instead of
the oil and substituting low-fat
cheese—a couple of changes
that you'll never notice in the
taste—will cut 100 calories
and 11 grams of fat out of this
recipe.

 VEG OUT

For a vegetarian version, substitute vegetable bouillon for
the chicken bouillon, leave out
the chicken, and garnish with
diced avocado.

BEEF STROGANOFF

J: As one of my all-time favorite dishes, I make this recipe all the time. It's best with fresh mushrooms, but I will admit that if I don't have any in the refrigerator (or if I'm feeling particularly lazy), I will make this with canned mushrooms and it's still yummy. When your friends think you've created a masterpiece, remember you don't have to tell them how easy it was.

SERVES 4

12 ounces uncooked noodles

1 large onion

6 ounces fresh mushrooms

1 pound sirloin or chuck steak

1 tablespoon canola oil

1 tablespoon cornstarch

2 teaspoons dried beef bouillon

1 1/2 cups water

1/2 cup sour cream

Bring a large saucepan of salted water to a boil and add the noodles. Cook over medium-high heat, stirring occasionally, for 10 minutes, or until al dente. Drain the noodles in a colander and keep warm.

Meanwhile, peel the onion and cut into 1/8-inch-thick slices. Remove and discard the ends of the mushroom stems and cut into 1/8- to 1/4-inch-thick slices. Remove and discard any visible fat from the meat and slice into 1/8- to 1/4-inch-thick strips.

Place the canola oil in a large sauté pan and add the onion and mushrooms. Cook over medium-high heat, stirring occasionally, for 10 minutes, or until the onions are lightly browned and soft. Add the meat and cook, stirring frequently, for 3 to 4 minutes, until the meat is browned. Combine the cornstarch and bouillon in a small bowl and slowly add the water, stirring until smooth. (If you put all the water in at once, the cornstarch will get lumpy.) Slowly stir the cornstarch mixture into the pan and bring to a boil. Remove from the heat and stir in the sour cream.

Serve immediately over the cooked noodles.

 FOOD FOR THOUGHT

Sirloin and chuck steak both work well in this recipe, so how do you decide which to use? Sirloin is more expensive, but it is much leaner and therefore has fewer calories. Chuck steak (also called pot roast) is inexpensive and very flavorful because it has more fat. So if you are on a tight budget, use the chuck steak. It is a tougher cut of meat that generally needs to cook for several hours to become tender, but if you slice it as thin as possible across (perpendicular to) the grain it will be very tender. If you are watching your calories, use the sirloin, fat-free sour cream, and cooking spray instead of oil for a low-calorie version that tastes as good as the original.

BARBECUE CHICKEN PITA PIZZA

J: Oh, Barbecue Chicken Pita Pizza, how I love thee! Okay, that might sound kind of weird, but try it and you'll know what I mean. These silly little pizzas are the easiest things in the world to make and most excellent to eat. In my opinion, that's the perfect combination. I like making them this way, but you could use almost any toppings you want.

1 pound boneless, skinless chicken breasts

4 pieces pita bread

1/4 cup barbecue sauce

1 tablespoon chopped fresh cilantro

1 1/2 cups shredded mozzarella or Jack cheese

Preheat the oven to 350°F.

Cut the chicken into 2-inch chunks and place in a small saucepan. Cover with water and cook over medium heat for 15 minutes, or until the chicken is cooked through. (Cut into one of the pieces to make sure there is no pink inside.) Remove from the heat and drain off the water.

Place the pita bread on a baking sheet and spread some of the barbecue sauce on each piece. Break the chicken into small pieces and arrange around the pita bread. Sprinkle with the cilantro and top with the cheese. Bake for 10 minutes, or until the cheese is melted. Remove from the oven and serve immediately.

 FOOD TRIVIA

According to the *Guinness Book of World Records*, the largest pizza order ever made was when a company ordered 13,386 pizzas from Little Caesar's to feed their 40,186 employees. Now that's what I call a pizza party!

 VEG OUT

If you haven't figured it out yet, this is the world's easiest recipe to adjust for vegetarians. Just leave out the chicken. If you want, you can add mushrooms, sliced tomatoes, or pretty much any vegetables you want.

TOMATO-BASIL PASTA

M: Here is another super simple dish that can be made in the time it takes to cook the pasta. You can use any type of pasta in this dish so feel free to swing out. I've used all different shapes, but my favorite was the pasta shaped like the state of Texas. It was so weird I had to buy it.

SERVES 4

1 pound uncooked pasta

2 cloves garlic

1 pound tomatoes (about 5 tomatoes)

1 (2/3-ounce) package fresh basil

8 ounces fresh mozzarella cheese (or 2 cups shredded)

2 tablespoons olive oil

Salt and pepper

Bring a large saucepan of salted water to a boil and add the pasta. Cook over medium-high heat, stirring occasionally, for 10 minutes, or until al dente. Drain the pasta in a colander and keep warm.

Meanwhile, peel the garlic and finely chop. Cut the tomatoes in quarters, remove and discard the stems and seeds, and cut into 1/2-inch pieces. Remove and discard the stems from the basil leaves and roughly chop so most of the pieces are 1/4 inch or less. Break the mozzarella into 1/4- to 1/2-inch pieces.

Heat the olive oil in a large sauté pan and add the tomatoes and garlic. Cook, stirring frequently for 5 minutes, or until the tomatoes are warmed through. Add the basil and stir until combined. Remove from the heat and stir in the hot pasta. Season with salt and pepper, stir in the mozzarella cheese, and serve immediately.

🥕 VEG OUT

Did you know that vegetarians have their own food pyramid? Each day vegetarians should have 6 to 11 servings of whole grain bread, cereal, pasta, and rice; 3 to 5 servings of vegetables; 2 to 4 servings of fruit; 2 to 3 servings of nuts, legumes, or meat alternatives; 2 to 3 servings of low-fat milk, yogurt, or cheese; and not very much vegetable oil, sugar, and salt.

EGGPLANT, TOMATO, AND MOZZARELLA STACKS

M: My boyfriend's mother made this dish when my family was visiting and we all fell in love with it. It's surprisingly simple, but the combination of flavors is amazing. She served it as a side dish, but we loved it so much that we make it as a meal now. Trust me, you have to try this recipe.

SERVES 4

2 eggplants

Salt and pepper

4 tomatoes

1 pound shredded mozzarella cheese

Preheat the oven to 350°F. Lightly coat a baking sheet with cooking spray.

Cut each eggplant into 12 slices and place on the baking sheet. Season with salt and pepper and bake for 20 minutes, or until the eggplant is soft.

Cut each tomato into 6 slices.

Top each of the eggplant slices with a slice of tomato and sprinkle with some of the mozzarella cheese. Place half of the eggplant stacks on top of the other half of the stacks so each one has six layers. Bake for 20 minutes, or until the cheese is lightly browned. Let cool for 5 minutes and serve.

FOOD TRIVIA

Eggplant belongs to the nightshade family, which includes the poisonous plants jimson weed and belladonna. Because of that, when it was first encountered by Europeans it gained the intimidating name of "mad apple." But more interesting to history geeks like me, it was first cultivated in America as one of the exotic plants in Thomas Jefferson's garden at Monticello. And if that's not enough, it was one of President Andrew Johnson's favorite foods.

🥕 VEG OUT

Contrary to popular belief, as long as vegetarians consume enough calories to maintain their weight, they can easily meet their protein needs by simply eating a varied diet. It's not necessary to plan combinations of foods, just to eat a variety of proteins throughout the day. Good protein sources are beans, lentils, tofu, nuts, seeds, chickpeas, and peas.

AVOIDING THE FRESHMAN FIFTEEN

One thing everyone hears about when they start college is the dreaded Freshman Fifteen. It's no wonder that with all the fast food choices and the freedom to eat truly whatever we want that it's easy to put on a few extra pounds. These recipes will help you balance out those late-night snacks. We've incorporated all the tricks we've learned about how to make dishes that are low in calories and fat but **still have a lot of flavor**. And, unlike the frozen dinners that are low-cal because you get about two tablespoons of food, these recipes actually make enough to fill you up. Once you get the hang of these recipes, you will be able to make simple adjustments to lower the fat and calories in just about anything you cook.

CHICKEN AND BROCCOLI STIR-FRY

J: This is a basic low-fat stir-fry recipe that can be adjusted almost any way you want. I often add pea pods, bean sprouts, celery, or whatever vegetables I happen to have on hand. One word of warning though; if you are making this for fewer than 4 people, cut the recipe down accordingly, as it doesn't reheat well. (And that's being kind.)

SERVES 4

RICE

2¼ cups water

1 cup rice

STIR-FRY

2 cloves garlic

1 pound boneless, skinless chicken breasts

4 green onions

4 cups broccoli florets

2 teaspoons dried chicken bouillon

1 cup water

1 tablespoon cornstarch

2 tablespoons low-sodium soy sauce

VEG OUT

This is another easy one to adapt for vegetarians. Leave out the chicken, substitute vegetable bouillon for the chicken bouillon, and add tofu or any vegetables you want.

To prepare the rice: Bring the water to a boil in a small saucepan. Stir in the rice, cover, and simmer over medium-low heat for 20 minutes, or until most of the water has been absorbed. Remove from the heat and let stand for 5 minutes.

To prepare the stir-fry: Peel the garlic and finely chop. Cut the chicken breasts into bite-size pieces and set aside. Trim the green onions, discarding the ends, and cut the white and about 1 inch of the green part into thin slices.

Place about 1 inch of water in a small saucepan and bring to a boil. Add the broccoli, cover, and cook over medium heat for 5 minutes, or until tender. (Alternatively, if you have a microwave, place the broccoli in a microwave-safe container and add a little water. Cover with plastic wrap or waxed paper and microwave on high heat for 5 minutes, or until tender.) Carefully drain off the water.

Coat a large skillet with cooking spray and place over medium-high heat. Add the garlic to the pan and cook, stirring constantly, for 30 seconds. Add the chicken and cook, stirring frequently, for 5 minutes, or until browned on all sides. Add the green onions and cook, stirring constantly, for 1 minute. Stir together the bouillon and water in a small bowl and add to the pan. Cook for 2 to 3 minutes, until it comes to a boil. Stir together the cornstarch and soy sauce in a small bowl until smooth and add to the pan. Stir until the sauce just begins to boil and remove from the heat. Add the broccoli and stir until it is coated with the sauce.

Place some of the rice on each plate, top with the stir-fry mixture, and serve immediately.

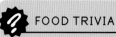

SPICY LETTUCE WRAPS

M: Although this recipe isn't hard, it does involve a fair amount of chopping. To me it's worth it because I love lettuce wraps, but the ones in restaurants are too high in calories. Using vegetables in place of some of the chicken dramatically cuts the calories in this dish, but it doesn't change the flavor. Fair warning though; if you've never used chili paste before, it's hot. You may want to start with half the amount and taste the sauce before adding more.

SERVES 4

SAUCE

1/2 cup low-sodium soy sauce

2/3 cup lime juice

2 tablespoons brown sugar

1 tablespoon chili paste

WRAPS

1/2 pound boneless, skinless chicken breast

1 onion

2 cloves garlic

2 small zucchini (about 1 pound)

1 pound fresh mushrooms

1 (8-ounce) can bamboo shoots

1 cucumber

1/2 red pepper

1 head iceberg or butter lettuce

1 teaspoon ground ginger

1/2 cup chopped peanuts

 VEG OUT

This recipe makes enough that you could probably just leave out the chicken and still have enough to serve four people, or you could add extra mushrooms or zucchini.

To make the sauce: Place the soy sauce, lime juice, brown sugar, and chili paste in a small bowl and stir until combined.

To make the wraps: Cut the chicken into 3- or 4-inch pieces. Coat a large sauté pan with cooking spray and add the chicken. Cook over medium-high heat, turning occasionally, for 10 minutes, or until the chicken is cooked through. (Cut into one of the pieces to make sure there is no pink inside.) Remove the chicken from the pan, let cool, and cut into 1/4-inch cubes.

Meanwhile, peel the onion and chop into 1/4-inch pieces. Peel and finely chop the garlic. Trim the zucchini and mushrooms, discarding the ends, and dice into 1/4-inch pieces. Drain the bamboo shoots and cut into 1/4-inch pieces. Peel the cucumber, cut into matchstick-size pieces (about 1/8 by 1/8 by 2 inches), and set aside for the garnish. Remove and discard the stem and seeds from the red pepper, cut into very thin slices, and set aside for the garnish. Separate the lettuce leaves from the head, wash, and let dry on paper towels. Place the lettuce, cucumber, and red pepper on a plate, cover with plastic wrap, and refrigerate until ready to serve.

Coat the sauté pan with more cooking spray and add the onion and garlic. Cook over medium-high heat, stirring occasionally, for 10 minutes, or until the onion is translucent. Add the zucchini and mushrooms, cover and cook over medium-high heat for 5 minutes. Add the chicken, bamboo shoots, ginger, and half of the sauce and cook, uncovered, for 2 to 3 minutes, until most of the liquid is absorbed.

Place the filling in a bowl and serve with the lettuce leaves, cucumber, red pepper, peanuts, and remaining sauce on the side. To assemble, place some of the filling inside a lettuce leaf. Arrange some of the cucumber and red pepper over the filling. Sprinkle with some of the chopped peanuts, drizzle with the sauce, and wrap up like a burrito.

LEMON CHICKEN WITH SAUTÉED SPINACH

J: This is a healthier and simpler version of one of my favorite recipes, chicken piccata. Usually I eat this dish with rice pilaf, but when I've overindulged, I save calories by skipping the breading and serving it on spinach. Even though I've never been a big spinach fan, it's yummy when you mix it with the lemon sauce.

SERVES 4

1 pound chicken breasts

Salt and pepper

2 teaspoons dried chicken bouillon

2 tablespoons cornstarch

1½ cups water

¼ cup lemon juice

1 pound frozen spinach

 FOOD FOR THOUGHT

I couldn't believe that this dish clocked in at an incredibly low 175 calories per serving. If you don't think it will be filling enough for you, add a cup of cooked rice and it's still only 335 calories. Or double the amount of chicken and it's only 290 calories. I've always loved this dish, but now I like it even better!

Cut each chicken breast in half lengthwise and season with salt and pepper. Coat a large sauté pan with cooking spray and place over medium-high heat. Add the chicken and cook for 5 minutes on each side, or until lightly browned.

Combine the bouillon and cornstarch in a small bowl and slowly stir in the water until smooth. (If you put all the water in at once, the cornstarch will get lumpy.) Pour the mixture into the pan and cook over medium heat, stirring occasionally, for 10 minutes, or until the mixture starts to thicken. Add the lemon juice and cook for 2 to 3 minutes, until the sauce just begins to boil.

Meanwhile, place about ½ inch of water in a small saucepan and bring to a boil. Add the spinach and cook, stirring occasionally, for 5 minutes, or until hot. (Alternatively, if you have a microwave, place the spinach in a microwave-safe bowl and microwave on high heat for 5 minutes, or until hot. Carefully remove the plastic wrap.) Press with the back of a spoon and drain off the water.

Divide the spinach between four plates, arrange the chicken over the spinach, and top with the sauce. Serve immediately.

CHICKEN CURRY

M: This is a delicious low-fat version of a standard curry dish. You might
think that low-fat means you won't be full, but with all the potatoes
and chicken in this easy-to-prepare meal, even big eaters will be satis-
fied. Curry can be a refreshing change especially if you've gotten
stuck in a culinary rut.

SERVES 4

1 pound boneless, skinless
chicken breasts

1 onion

1 pound potatoes

2 tablespoons low-sodium
soy sauce

1 teaspoon dried chicken
bouillon

1/2 cup water

2 teaspoons curry powder

2 cups frozen peas

1/2 cup plain low-fat yogurt

Cut the chicken into bite-size pieces. Peel the onion, cut in half, and thinly slice. Peel the potatoes and cut into 3/4-inch cubes.

Generously spray a large sauté pan with cooking spray. Add the chicken, onion, and potatoes and cook over medium-high heat, stirring frequently, for 5 minutes. Stir together the soy sauce, bouillon, water, and curry powder and add to the pan. Cover and cook for 10 minutes, or until a fork slides easily into the potatoes. Add the peas and cook for 2 minutes. Remove the pan from the heat and stir in the yogurt. Serve immediately.

 FOOD TRIVIA

Curry powder is a widely varied mixture of spices that was developed by the British during their colonial rule of India as a way to approximate the taste of Indian cuisine at home. Curry powders usually include cumin, coriander, turmeric, and fenugreek, but some may also have ginger, garlic, clove, mustard seed, nutmeg, red pepper, or black pepper. Each British house-hold developed its own recipe and kept it a closely guarded secret.

SHRIMP LINGUINE MARINARA

M: Although we college kids are known for our love of pasta because it's cheap and easy to make, that doesn't mean it can't also taste great and be low in calories. This dish is a perfect example of that. Shrimp Linguine Marinara tastes like an extravagant indulgence, but it's only about 400 calories per serving.

SERVES 4

12 ounces uncooked linguine

4 cloves garlic

1 pound peeled and deveined raw shrimp

1 teaspoon crushed red pepper

2 (15-ounce) cans crushed tomatoes

1 teaspoon Italian seasoning

Salt and pepper

 BARGAIN SHOPPER

Shrimp sizes and prices are determined by the number of shrimp per pound. They are usually packaged as 11/20, 21/30, 31/40, 41/50, or 51/60 sizes. That means that the 11/20 will have 11 to 20 shrimp per pound. The larger shrimp are impressive, but at about $20 per pound, the price is prohibitive. So unless you are really trying to impress someone, the smaller 41/50 or 51/60 shrimp are a much better buy, often going on sale for $4 to $5 per pound.

Bring a large saucepan of salted water to a boil and add the linguine. Cook over medium-high heat, stirring occasionally, for 12 to 15 minutes, until al dente. Drain the linguine in a colander and keep warm.

Meanwhile, peel the garlic and finely chop.

Coat a large sauté pan with cooking spray and place over medium-high heat. Add the shrimp and cook for 2 to 3 minutes on each side until just cooked. (They will turn pink and curl up when they are done. Do not overcook or the shrimp will become tough and chewy.) Remove the shrimp from the pan and add the garlic, crushed red pepper, tomatoes, and Italian seasoning. Cook for 10 minutes, or until it begins to thicken. Season with salt and pepper. Stir in the shrimp and serve over the linguine.

BEEF ENCHILADAS

J: I know you're thinking, "Yeah, it's low-cal because I only get one measly enchilada." Not true. Okay, partially true, you only get one enchilada per serving, but they're really big. By making larger enchiladas, you can pack them with all the good stuff and still save a couple hundred calories from skipping the extra tortillas.

SERVES 4

1 small onion

1/2 pound extra-lean ground beef

2 teaspoons Mexican seasoning

2 cups salsa

1 (4-ounce) can diced green chiles

1 (15-ounce) can pinto or black beans

4 6-inch low-fat flour tortillas

1/2 cup low-fat shredded cheddar or Jack cheese

Preheat the oven to 350°F. Lightly spray an 8-inch baking pan with cooking spray.

Peel the onion and chop into 1/4- to 1/2-inch pieces. Place the onion and ground beef in a large sauté pan and cook over medium-high heat for 10 minutes, or until completely browned. Drain off any grease and add the Mexican seasoning, 1 cup of the salsa, and the green chiles with the juice. Drain the liquid from the beans and stir into the mixture. Cook for 7 to 10 minutes, until the liquid is absorbed. Spoon one quarter of the meat mixture into the center of each tortilla and roll them up. Place the enchiladas seam side down in the pan, cover with the remaining 1 cup of salsa, and top with the cheese. Bake for 15 minutes, or until the cheese is melted. Serve immediately.

 FOOD FOR THOUGHT

Mexican food has a reputation for being high in fat. Perhaps that's true of the food you buy in restaurants, but with just a few minor adjustments you easily can change your favorite dishes into low-fat meals. Using low-fat cheese, sour cream, and tortillas, fat-free refried or black beans, and lean meats, you can make a healthier version of just about any Mexican dish and you won't even notice the difference.

SZECHUAN CHICKEN

M: This recipe may look complicated because it has a lot of ingredients, but it's not. You can prepare the whole dish in the time it takes to cook the rice. I use water chestnuts and pea pods in the recipe, but this is one of those dishes where just about any vegetables you happen to have in the refrigerator will work fine.

RICE

2 1/4 cups water

1 cup rice

CHICKEN

1 pound boneless, skinless chicken breasts

3 tablespoons cornstarch

4 cloves garlic

4 green onions

2 teaspoons dried chicken bouillon

1/3 cup low-sodium soy sauce

1 1/2 tablespoons white wine vinegar

1 cup water

1 teaspoon sugar

1 cup pea pods

1 (8-ounce) can sliced water chestnuts

1/2 teaspoon crushed red pepper

To prepare the rice: Place the water in a saucepan and bring to a boil. Add the rice, cover, and cook over low heat for 20 minutes, or until most of the liquid is absorbed. Remove from the heat and let stand for 5 minutes, or until all of the water is absorbed.

To prepare the chicken: Cut the chicken into 1-inch cubes. Place the chicken in a bowl, add the cornstarch, and toss until coated. Peel the garlic, finely chop, and add to the bowl with the chicken. Trim the green onions, discarding the ends, and slice the white and about 2 inches of the green part into 1/2-inch pieces on the diagonal. Set aside.

Coat a large sauté pan with cooking spray and place over medium-high heat. Add the chicken and cook, stirring constantly, for 5 minutes, or until lightly browned. Add the bouillon, soy sauce, vinegar, water, and sugar and stir well. Cover and cook for 3 to 4 minutes, until the chicken is cooked through. (Cut into one of the pieces to make sure there is no pink inside.) Add the green onion, pea pods, water chestnuts, and crushed red pepper and cook, uncovered, for 2 minutes, or until the onions just begin to wilt.

Place some of the rice in the center of each plate, top with some of the chicken mixture, and serve immediately.

VEG OUT

Although you could just substitute vegetable bouillon for the chicken bouillon and extra vegetables for the chicken, I think this is better if you substitute tofu for the chicken. The tofu will absorb some of the heat from the sauce and is really tasty.

 VEG OUT

A vegetarian diet is known to have a wide range of health benefits. Research has shown vegetarians suffer less heart disease, hypertension, obesity, diabetes, various cancers, diverticular disease, gallstones, kidney stones, and osteoporosis. So next time someone hassles you about being a vegetarian, list all those reasons. That will shut them up.

VEGETARIAN CHILI

M: This chili is so tasty that your carnivore friends may not even notice it doesn't have meat. It makes a lot, so if you have leftovers, freeze individual portions in resealable bags. For a quick meal, just nuke one and eat it my favorite way: poured over a baked potato.

SERVES 6

1 onion

1 red pepper

2 stalks celery

1 clove garlic

1/4 cup water

2 small zucchini (about 1 pound)

Salt and pepper

2 (14-ounce) cans diced tomatoes

1 (6-ounce) can tomato paste

2 tablespoons chili powder

2 (15-ounce) cans kidney beans

Peel the onion, cut into 1/2-inch pieces, and place in a large saucepan. Cut the pepper in half and remove and discard the stem and seeds. Cut into 1/2-inch pieces and add to the pan. Trim the celery and discard the ends. Cut in half lengthwise and then cut into 1/2-inch pieces and add to the pan. Peel the garlic, finely chop, and place in the pan. Add the water to the pan and cook over medium heat for 5 minutes. Trim the zucchini and discard the ends. Cut in quarters lengthwise and then cut into 1/2-inch pieces and add to the pan. Cook for 10 minutes. Season with salt and pepper. Add the tomatoes, tomato paste, chili powder, and undrained kidney beans and cook over low heat for 45 minutes for the flavors to meld. Season with salt, pepper, and additional chili powder, if desired, and serve warm.

 FOOD TRIVIA

Onions were actually objects of worship in ancient Egypt. They thought the circle-within-a-circle structure symbolized eternity. Mummies have frequently been found with onions in their pelvic regions, thorax, flattened against the ears and in front of the eyes. Egyptologists hypothesize that it was perhaps believed the strong scent and/or magical powers of onions would prompt the dead to breathe again. After being buried with onions for all that time, I just hope they don't breathe on me.

COUSCOUS-STUFFED PEPPERS

M: I created this recipe when I was living in France, where they use a lot of couscous. Since I love peppers I started experimenting with different combinations and found that there really is no bad combination. You can use any vegetables and even throw in some cooked meat, if you have some that needs to be used up.

SERVES 4

1 cup couscous

1 cup water

1 onion

6 ounces fresh mushrooms

1 carrot

1/2 cup frozen peas

Salt and pepper

4 red or green peppers

 FOOD FOR THOUGHT

At first glance mushrooms seem rather insignificant nutritionally. In fact, the only numbers on the nutrition labels that aren't zeros are 20 calories and 3 grams of carbs. But, if you dig a little further you will find that they are actually an excellent source of selenium, a mineral that works closely with vitamin E to produce antioxidants that can decrease the risk of cancer and other diseases of aging. They also contain a significant amount of potassium, which helps maintain normal heart rhythm, fluid balance, muscle, and nerve function. And all this time I just thought they tasted good.

Preheat the oven to 375°F.

Bring the water to a boil in a small saucepan and stir in the couscous. Remove from the heat and let stand for 5 minutes.

Peel the onion and cut into 1/2-inch pieces. Cut the ends of the stems off the mushrooms and thinly slice. Peel the carrot and cut into 1/4-inch cubes.

Generously coat a sauté pan with cooking spray and add the onion, mushrooms, and carrot. Cook over medium heat, stirring frequently, for 10 minutes, or until the mushrooms are soft. Remove from the heat, add the couscous and peas, and stir until combined. Season with salt and pepper.

Cut the tops off of the peppers and remove and discard the seeds. Place the peppers in a baking pan, trimming the bottoms, if necessary, to make them stand up. Fill the peppers with the couscous mixture and cover the pan with aluminum foil. Bake for 30 to 40 minutes, until the peppers are soft. Remove from the oven and serve immediately.

HUMMUS

BACON-
WRAPPED
DATES

FETA-
STUFFED
CHERRY
TOMATOES

SPINACH
PHYLLO
TARTS

TZATZIKI

BAKLAVA

TOGA PARTY

We can be thankful to citizens of ancient Greece for numerous things, including coined money, thermometers, central heating, ship anchors, catapults, steam engines, levers, and several schools of philosophy. Along with their ability to work and think hard was their love for playing hard, typified by the *symposium*, or Greek drinking party.

Although the typical *symposium* would be after dinner, when only grapes or cheese would be eaten, we've taken some liberties and included our favorite versions of **typical Greek foods**. Some are quicker to make than others, but all are delicious, as our friends can tell you. And for some added fun, typically Greek or not, we've thrown in some ways to spice up the party. You can try for a sophisticated, subdued party, but if your friends are anything like ours it's more likely to end up loud and slightly bawdy. Either way, just remember, everything's more interesting when you're wearing a toga.

HUMMUS

J: This is a most excellent appetizer and it couldn't be easier to make. You just put everything in the blender and it's done in about 30 seconds. You can't beat that.

1 (15-ounce) can chickpeas

3 cloves garlic

1 teaspoon Mexican seasoning

1/4 cup lemon juice

1/3 cup olive oil

6 pieces pita bread

Drain the chickpeas and place in a blender with the garlic, Mexican seasoning, lemon juice, and olive oil. Purée for 30 seconds, or until the mixture is smooth.

Cut each piece of pita bread into 8 wedges and serve on a plate with the hummus on the side.

TZATZIKI

J: What is tzatziki you ask? It's a cucumber sauce that they serve as a spread for pita bread in every Greek restaurant. And, if that doesn't help, it's the white sauce that they put on gyros. If you still don't know what I mean, make it and you'll find out.

1 cucumber

3 green onions

2 cloves garlic

4 ounces feta cheese

2 cups sour cream

Salt and pepper

6 pieces pita bread

Peel the cucumber, cut in half lengthwise, and scrape out the seeds with a spoon. Cut each piece in half again lengthwise and cut into very thin slices. If you have time, place the cucumber in a colander, sprinkle with salt, and let stand in the sink or over a bowl for 2 to 3 hours. (The salt will leech the water from the cucumbers so the sauce won't get runny. If you need to skip this step because you don't have time, decrease the sour cream by 1/2 cup.)

Trim the green onions, discarding the ends, and cut all of the white and about 1 inch of the green parts into thin slices. Peel the garlic and finely chop.

Place the feta cheese and sour cream in a bowl and stir until combined. Stir in the cucumber, onions, and garlic and season with salt and pepper.

Cut each piece of pita bread into 8 wedges and serve on a large plate with the sauce on the side.

 SETTING THE SCENE

Decorations are not a necessity, but if you want to make it a little more fun, put pillows all around and insist that everyone lounge on the floor. (Plus it makes you look like not such a bad host/ hostess if you don't have a lot of chairs.) Put all of the food out on a low coffee table with a big bowl of grapes and cheese, and before you know it people will be trying to get everyone else to fan them and serve them grapes.

BACON-WRAPPED DATES

J: I am usually not a particular fan of dates. Normally, I think they are too sweet and sticky, but in this dish the smokiness of the bacon offsets some of the sweetness and the combination is delicious. They're also easy and fast to make.

MAKES ABOUT
30 PIECES

1/2 pound bacon

1/2 pound pitted dates

3/4 cup apricot or peach jam

Preheat the oven to 400°F.

Cut the bacon slices into thirds. Wrap a piece of bacon around each date and secure by sticking a toothpick through the bacon and into the date.

Stir the jam vigorously for 1 minute, or until it loosens up enough to thinly coat the dates. (Alternatively, if you have a microwave, place the jam in a microwave-safe bowl and microwave on high for 30 seconds, or until barely warm.)

Dip the wrapped dates in the jam and place on a baking sheet. Bake for 20 to 25 minutes, until the bacon is cooked. Place the dates on a serving plate and serve warm.

FETA-STUFFED CHERRY TOMATOES

J: These aren't hard to make, but it does take a while to clean out the insides of all of the tomatoes. The good news is that they can be made up to a day ahead and the taste is most definitely worth the effort.

MAKES 32 TOMATOES

32 cherry tomatoes

4 ounces cream cheese, softened

1/4 cup sour cream

4 ounces feta cheese

2 tablespoons chopped fresh chives or green onion

1/4 teaspoon Italian seasoning

Cut the tops off the cherry tomatoes. Run a small knife around the inside of the tomatoes, remove and discard the seeds, keeping the tomatoes whole.

Place the cream cheese in a bowl and stir until smooth. Add the sour cream, feta cheese, chives, and Italian seasoning and stir until smooth. Spoon some of the cheese mixture into each of the tomatoes and arrange on a serving plate. Cover with plastic wrap and refrigerate until ready to serve.

SPINACH PHYLLO TARTS

J: Okay, I won't lie to you, these take a while to make, but they're
so delectable and quintessentially Greek that it's worth
the time it takes. You can make these several hours ahead
and serve them at room temperature or you can put them
together and just bake them right before you serve them.

8 ounces frozen spinach

4 ounces cream cheese, softened

4 ounces feta cheese

1 egg

1 teaspoon salt

8 ounces phyllo dough, thawed

1/2 cup melted butter

Let the spinach sit at room temperature for about 30 minutes, until thawed. (Alternatively, if you have a microwave, place the spinach in a microwave-safe bowl and cook on high for 2 minutes, or until thawed.) Drain, pressing on the spinach with the back of a spoon to remove any excess water. Add the cream cheese and stir until smooth. Add the feta cheese, egg, and salt and stir until evenly distributed.

Preheat the oven to 375°F.

Unroll the phyllo dough, place on a flat surface, and immediately cover with barely damp paper towels. (Make sure to cover the phyllo every time you take a sheet or it will dry out.) Lay one sheet of phyllo on a work surface and brush the entire surface with some of the butter. Top with another sheet of phyllo and brush with butter. Continue the process until you have 3 layers of phyllo. Cut the phyllo into 6 strips and place a rounded teaspoon of the filling at the bottom end of each strip. Pull the corner of one phyllo strip up over the filling to form a triangle. Fold the triangle up and over and continue folding the triangle over, making tight flag folds, until you reach the end of the strip, being careful to keep the corners tight. (You should start and end with a triangle.) Brush the loose end of the phyllo with butter and press to seal. Place the triangle on a baking sheet, seam side down, and repeat with the remaining strips.

Brush the tops of the triangles with butter. Repeat the entire process with the remaining phyllo and filling. Bake for 30 to 35 minutes, until golden brown.

Place on a serving platter and serve warm or at room temperature.

DRESSING THE PART

Obviously to be a toga party everyone should wear a toga. To make a toga either use a sheet or a large piece of fabric (if it is larger than a standard twin-size sheet, fold it in half unless you're really tall (or if you're a midget like Megan, fold it in quarters). Contrary to popular opinion, ancient Greeks wore other garments under their togas, so remember being scantily clad is not a requirement. Either wrap the sheet around your waist once, pin it, and then throw the rest over your shoulder and pin it again, or wrap the sheet around you, cross the two top corners of the sheet under one arm, and then cross the rest over your shoulder. Go barefoot or wear sandals. You can make your own laurels by tying any kind of green stuff (real or fake) into a wreath to go on your head, although we suggest you ask before taking it from someone's yard.

BAKLAVA

J: No toga party would be complete without baklava. Of course,
you could just go out and buy baklava, but this version is better
than anything I've ever tried and is not difficult at all. It's got
the great flavor of the nuts and honey without being too sweet.

SYRUP

1/2 cup sugar

1 cup water

1 tablespoon lemon juice

1/2 cup honey

1/2 teaspoon cinnamon

BAKLAVA

3 cups finely chopped
walnuts

1/4 cup sugar

1 teaspoon cinnamon

8 ounces phyllo dough,
thawed

3/4 cup melted butter

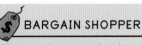 BARGAIN SHOPPER

Nuts can be expensive, but
there are ways to make it a little
easier on your wallet. Chopped
walnuts usually come in 1/2 cup
packages so you would need
6 packages for this recipe. You
can buy a large bag of walnut
pieces and chop them with a
knife or in the blender for about
half the cost.

To prepare the syrup: Place the sugar and water in a small
saucepan and cook over high heat until the mixture begins to
boil. Reduce to medium-low heat and simmer for 15 minutes.
Add the lemon juice, honey, and cinnamon and cook, stirring
occasionally, for 5 minutes. Remove from the heat and cool
completely.

To prepare the baklava: Preheat the oven to 375°F.

Combine the walnuts, sugar, and cinnamon in a bowl.
Unroll the phyllo dough, place on a flat surface, and immediately cover with barely damp paper towels. (Make sure to
cover the phyllo every time you take a sheet or it will dry out.)
Cut the stack of phyllo sheets into a 9 by 13-inch rectangle,
discarding the excess.

Lay one sheet of phyllo in the bottom of a 9 by 13-inch
baking pan and brush the entire surface with some of the butter. Top with another sheet of phyllo and brush with butter.
Continue the process until you have a layer of 4 phyllo sheets.
Sprinkle with 1/2 cup of the nut mixture and continue layering,
alternating layers of 2 sheets of buttered phyllo with 1/2 cup of
nuts. Top with 4 sheets of buttered phyllo, making sure the top
phyllo sheet is generously buttered. With a serrated knife, cut
the stacks into 48 squares and bake for 30 to 35 minutes, until
golden brown. (The baklava must be cut before baking. Once
the phyllo dough is cooked it gets crispy and will crumble
apart when you try to cut it.)

Pour the cooled syrup over the hot baklava and allow to
cool completely. Arrange the baklava on a serving plate and
serve at room temperature.

CHEAP
EATS

We know all about how tight money can be when you are in school, but eating ramen or boxed macaroni and cheese every night is not the answer. Each of these recipes serves four people for about the cost of one fast food meal. But, don't be put off because these dishes are made using cheap ingredients, they're so tasty that you'll want to make them even if you aren't on a tight budget. Besides, even when you have money it's much more fun to spend it on clothes or going out . . . er, that is, buying books.

POTATO PANCAKES

SERVES 4

J: When I suggested potato pancakes for this chapter, my mom questioned whether college students would own blenders. I foolishly said, "Even the guys next door who have one fry pan and eat with plastic silverware have a blender." I quickly added, "You know, to make smoothies." I don't think she bought the smoothie thing, but the recipe stayed. These crispy potato pancakes are a yummy dinner plain or with applesauce or sour cream.

4 medium potatoes

1 small onion

1/4 cup milk

2 eggs

3 tablespoons flour

1 teaspoon salt

1/4 teaspoon baking powder

Canola oil for frying

Applesauce (optional)

Sour cream (optional)

VEG OUT

If you're a vegetarian, you are in excellent company. A few of the more famous vegetarians in history are Albert Einstein, Albert Schweitzer, Benjamin Franklin, Henry David Thoreau, Louisa May Alcott, Susan B. Anthony, and Vincent Van Gogh.

Peel the potatoes and cut into 1/2- to 3/4-inch pieces. (You should have about 3 cups.)

Peel the onion and cut into quarters.

Place the potatoes, onion, milk, eggs, flour, salt, and baking powder in the blender and pulse for about 20 seconds, until all of the potatoes have gone through the blades. (Stop as soon as you see the last of the potatoes go through the blades.)

Pour about 2 tablespoons of oil into a frying pan and place over medium-high heat for 30 seconds, or until a tiny drop of water sizzles as soon as it hits the oil. (Use caution when testing the oil: too much water can cause the hot oil to splash violently.) Pour the batter into the pan using about 1/3 cup for each pancake. (You can make them any size you want, but it's easier to turn them if they are about as wide as your spatula.) Cook for 5 minutes, or until golden brown. Turn the pancakes over and cook for 2 to 3 minutes, until lightly browned and the centers are set. Repeat the process with the remaining batter, adding new oil to the pan for each batch. Serve warm with applesauce and sour cream.

SPAGHETTI CARBONARA

M: Okay, I know this isn't authentic carbonara, but eliminating the cream cuts the calories and reduces the cost. As long as it still has that exquisite bacon and Parmesan cheese flavor, I'm all for fewer calories and less money. This is another super simple recipe with generous portions that reheat well.

SERVES 4

1 pound uncooked spaghetti

12 ounces bacon

2 cloves garlic

4 eggs

1/2 cup milk

1/2 cup grated Parmesan cheese

Salt and pepper

Bring a large saucepan of salted water to a boil and add the spaghetti. Cook for 10 minutes, or until al dente. Drain the spaghetti in a colander and keep warm.

Meanwhile, cut the bacon widthwise into 1/4-inch strips and cook in a large sauté pan over medium-high heat, stirring frequently, for 20 minutes, or until it just starts to get crisp. (If it is too crisp, it will break into tiny pieces when you mix it with the pasta.) Drain off the bacon grease.

Peel the garlic and finely chop. Add the garlic to the bacon and cook for 2 minutes, or until the garlic just begins to brown.

Beat the eggs in a small bowl until completely combined. Add the milk and Parmesan cheese and stir well. Add the hot spaghetti and egg mixture to the pan, remove from the heat, and stir until the noodles are coated and the eggs are cooked. Season generously with salt and pepper and serve immediately.

 FOOD TRIVIA

When I looked into the history of carbonara, the stories ranged from ascribing its ancient origins with the Romans to identifying it as a more recent invention developed as a way to use bacon and eggs bought on the black market in Italy from American service person- nel stationed there during the Second World War. But my favorite was an explanation of the name *alla carbonara*, which means "in the manner of the coal miners." According to legend, the dish was popular with Italian miners because the few ingredients could easily be carried or, in the case of eggs, pocketed from henhouses on the way to work. A simple campfire in the woods was all that was needed to make an elegant meal.

WHAT'S-IN-THE-FRIDGE FRITTATA

M: If your budget looks anything like mine, you'll be eating this a lot. This
is an ideal way to use up the leftovers in your fridge. Since most items
need to be cooked before going in a frittata anyway, leftovers are
perfect candidates. Onion, zucchini, tomato, broccoli, cheese, ham,
potatoes, chicken, rice, and pasta—anything goes. Be bold and expand
your horizons. Don't be afraid to venture beyond typical omelet ingredients. And if you don't have enough leftovers, open a can of corn and
chop up some corn tortillas and toss those in.

SERVES 4

8 eggs

1/2 cup milk

1/2 teaspoon salt

1/4 teaspoon pepper

4 cups leftovers

Preheat the oven to 350°F. Lightly coat an 8-inch baking pan
with butter or cooking spray.

Beat the eggs, milk, salt, and pepper in a bowl until well
combined. Distribute the leftovers evenly in the pan and pour
in the eggs. Bake for 45 to 50 minutes, until a knife inserted in
the center comes out clean. Remove from the oven and serve
immediately.

 FOOD TRIVIA

A frittata is the Italian version
of an omelet, but instead of
the ingredients being folded
into the middle they are mixed
right into the eggs, so it's
actually easier to make. Frit-
tatas are usually started on the
stove and finished in the oven,
but you have to have pans
with metal handles. Since I
don't, I learned to adapt. This
version is the same principle
as a frittata, but you don't
have to worry about melting
the handles on your pans.

MACARONI AND CHEESE WITH HAM

M: You're in college now so it's time to break away from boxed mac 'n' cheese and try the real thing. It's not hard to make and once you realize how creamy and cheesy the homemade version tastes, you'll never go back to that boxed stuff. We added ham to this dish, but you could make it without the ham or with cooked chicken or broccoli. Hey, don't knock it 'til you've tried it. Who doesn't love cheesy broccoli?

1 pound uncooked macaroni

2 tablespoons butter

2 tablespoons flour

2 cups milk

1 pound sliced American cheese

1/2 pound lean ham

Bring a large saucepan of salted water to a boil. Add the macaroni and cook, stirring occasionally, for 7 to 10 minutes, until al dente. Drain the macaroni in a colander.

Preheat the oven to 350°F. Lightly coat a large baking dish or pan with oil or cooking spray.

Melt the butter in the same saucepan over medium heat. Add the flour and stir constantly until the mixture starts to bubble. (Do not let the mixture brown or your sauce will have a brown tinge to it.) Add about 1/2 cup of the milk and stir until smooth. Add the remaining milk and cook, stirring frequently, for 10 to 15 minutes, until it comes to a boil. Remove the pan from the heat, add the cheese, and stir until the cheese is completely melted.

Cut the ham into 1/2-inch cubes and stir into the cheese sauce. Add the macaroni and stir gently until it is completely coated with the cheese.

Place the mixture in a large baking dish and bake for 25 to 30 minutes, until the cheese is bubbly. Remove from the oven and serve immediately.

 FOOD TRIVIA

It seems that our humble macaroni and cheese began as food for royalty. The first recipe for it appeared in a cookbook called *Forme of Cury*, compiled in 1390 by the master cooks of King Richard II, and was later presented to Queen Elizabeth. I love these old recipes:

> *Take and make a thin foil of dowh, and kerve it on peces, and cast hem on boiling water and seeth it wele. Take chese and grate it and butter cast bynethen and above as losyns. And serve forth.*

BLACK BEANS AND RICE WITH RECAITO

M: This is the epitome of college budget dishes. It's yummy, cheap, easy, and it even has complete protein. (Your mom will be so proud.) Recaito is a cilantro-flavored Mexican sauce that can be found in the Mexican food aisle in most grocery stores. You could also make your own by chopping up fresh cilantro, green pepper, onion, and garlic, but at $1.25 for enough to make this six times, I go for the jar.

SERVES 4

2¼ cups water

1 cup rice

1 tablespoon olive oil

3 tablespoons recaito

2 (15-ounce) cans black beans

1 (15-ounce) can diced tomatoes

Place the water in a saucepan and bring to a boil. Add the rice, cover, and cook over low heat for 20 minutes, or until most of the water is absorbed. Remove from the heat and let stand for 5 minutes, or until all of the water is absorbed.

Meanwhile, place the olive oil in a saucepan over medium heat and add the recaito. Cook for 2 minutes, or until bubbly. Drain the beans and add to the pan. Add the tomatoes with their juice and stir well. Cook for 15 minutes, or until most of the liquid is absorbed, and serve hot over the rice.

 FOOD FOR THOUGHT

Served separately, beans and rice lack the components necessary to make a complete protein. But, when combined their protein value is equal to fish, poultry, or red meat. Dried beans are also rich in iron and their high fiber content can help reduce blood cholesterol.

OVEN-FRIED CHICKEN WITH POTATO WEDGES

J: This is an easy way to make tasty fried chicken without any of the mess. I like chicken legs, so whenever they are on sale I buy one of those huge packages with about twelve in it and make them all. It is never a problem to get rid of leftover fried chicken.

SERVES 4

1/2 cup flour

1 teaspoon salt

1/2 teaspoon pepper

1 teaspoon paprika

3 to 4 pounds bone-in chicken pieces (about 8 pieces)

2 tablespoons butter

1 1/2 pounds potatoes (about 5 medium)

1 tablespoon canola oil

Salt

Preheat the oven to 400°F. Generously coat a 9 by 13-inch baking pan with oil or cooking spray.

Place the flour, salt, pepper, and paprika in a shallow bowl or resealable bag and mix well. Coat the chicken pieces thoroughly with the flour and place in the pan. Place a small piece of butter on top of each piece of chicken and bake for 45 to 50 minutes, until golden brown.

Meanwhile, cut each potato into 8 wedges and place on a baking sheet. Drizzle the oil over the potatoes and toss until completely coated. Season with salt and bake for 30 minutes, or until lightly browned.

Place some of the chicken and potato wedges on each plate and serve immediately.

 FOOD FOR THOUGHT

By simply removing the skin from the chicken, skipping the butter, and using cooking spray on the potatoes instead of oil, you can save 275 calories and a whopping 33 grams of fat. I think that speaks for itself.

POTATO AND BACON CASSEROLE

M: This is based on a French dish popular during the cold winter months. SERVES 4
They use Reblochon, a super delicious stinky cheese, but since it's hard
to find here (and expensive), I used Swiss instead. This is so delicious
that I cut it into quarters as soon as it comes out of the oven to avoid
the fights over who got more. (And I'm not kidding about that.)

2 pounds potatoes (about 7)

2 tablespoons butter

3 tablespoons flour

1 cup milk

1/2 pound bacon

1 onion

1 cup sour cream

2 cups shredded Swiss
cheese

Preheat the oven to 375°F. Lightly butter or spray a 9 by
13-inch baking pan.

Cut the potatoes into 1/16- to 1/8-inch-thick slices and
arrange half of the slices in the bottom of the pan. Cut the butter into small pieces and distribute over the potatoes. Sprinkle
the flour over the layer and top with the remaining potatoes.
Pour the milk over the potatoes and bake for 45 minutes, or
until a knife slides easily into the center.

Meanwhile, cut the bacon into 1/2-inch-wide pieces and
cook in a sauté pan over medium-high heat for 10 minutes, or
until the bacon just begins to get brown. Peel the onion and
chop into 1/4- to 1/2-inch pieces. Add the onion to the pan and
cook for 10 minutes, or until the onion is translucent. Remove
from the pan and drain on paper towels.

Carefully remove the potatoes from the oven. Spread
the sour cream over the cooked potatoes and cover with the
bacon mixture. Sprinkle the cheese evenly over the bacon
and bake for 15 minutes more, or until the cheese is melted.
Remove from the oven and serve immediately.

 FOOD TRIVIA

Back in the sixteenth century,
pork was expensive and when
commoners could afford it
they felt quite special. When
visitors came over, they would
hang up their bacon to show
off. It was a sign of wealth that
the man could "bring home
the bacon." They would cut
off a little to share with guests
and they would all sit around
and "chew the fat." Ewww.
I hope they cooked it first.

CHICKEN PASTA PRIMAVERA

M: This is another dish that you can easily adjust to suit your tastes. You can use any vegetables you like. When your budget is squeaking tight, make it with just peas and carrots. But when you have a little more wiggle room, try it with red peppers, zucchini, and sugar snap peas.

SERVES 4

1 pound uncooked pasta

3 carrots

2 boneless, skinless chicken breasts

6 ounces fresh mushrooms

1 tablespoon canola oil

1 cup frozen peas

3/4 cup milk

1/2 cup grated Parmesan cheese

Bring a large saucepan of salted water to a boil and add the pasta. Cook for 10 minutes, or until al dente. Drain the pasta in a colander and keep warm.

Peel the carrots and slice into 1/4-inch-thick rings. Place the carrot rings in a small saucepan and completely cover with water. Cook over medium heat for 15 minutes, or until the carrots are just soft. (Alternatively, if you have a microwave, place in a microwave-safe bowl and add a little water. Cover loosely with waxed paper or plastic wrap and cook on high heat for 6 to 7 minutes, until just soft.) Carefully drain off the water.

Cut the chicken into bite-size pieces. Cut the ends off the mushroom stems, discard, and thinly slice the mushrooms.

Place the oil in a large sauté pan over medium-high heat and add the chicken and mushrooms. Cook, stirring frequently, for 10 minutes, or until the mushrooms are golden brown.

Add the peas and milk to the pan and cook for 5 minutes, or until the milk is hot and starts to steam. (Do not let the milk boil.) Add the Parmesan cheese and stir until the sauce is smooth. Remove the pan from the heat, add the carrots and pasta, and stir until combined. Serve immediately.

💡 FOOD FOR THOUGHT

Carrots are said to fight cancer, lower cholesterol, and boost the immune system. They contain vitamins A, B, C, D, E, potassium, magnesium, and beta-carotene. Contrary to most other vegetables, a cooked carrot is more nutritious than its raw counterpart. Cooking breaks down a carrot's fiber, making the beta-carotene and sugars easier to digest. And just FYI, Mel Blanc, the voice of Bugs Bunny, was not very fond of carrots.

VEG OUT

Here's a tough one: leave out the chicken. You can add extra veggies if you want, but it's not necessary.

BEEF CHIMICHANGAS

J: These are one of my favorite things to order in a restaurant, so when we figured out how to make them at home, I was super excited. They are actually pretty easy to make, which is even better. For an even lower-budget option, leave out the ground beef, use the whole can of refried beans, and add an extra cup of cheese.

SERVES 4

1 green pepper

1 onion

1 clove garlic

1 pound ground beef

1/2 cup salsa

1/2 teaspoon salt

1 cup refried beans

1 cup shredded Jack cheese

4 10-inch flour tortillas

Canola oil for frying

Salsa

Sour cream

 VEG OUT

Tofu chimichangas may sound weird, but they're surprisingly tasty. Just sauté the green pepper and onion in cooking spray or a tablespoon of canola oil. Cut an 8-ounce package of tofu into 1/4-inch cubes and stir it in with the beans and cheese.

Remove and discard the stem and seeds from the pepper and chop into 1/4- to 1/2-inch pieces. Peel the onion and chop into 1/4- to 1/2-inch pieces. Peel the garlic, finely chop, and place in a large sauté pan with the onion, green pepper, and ground beef. Cook over medium-high heat for 10 minutes, or until the ground beef is no longer pink. Drain any grease from the pan, stir in the salsa and salt, and cook for 1 minute. Remove from the heat and stir in the refried beans and cheese.

Place the flour tortillas on a flat surface and spoon one quarter of the meat mixture in the center of each tortilla. Fold in the sides and then fold over the top and bottom to form the chimichangas. (You can weave a toothpick through the flaps to keep them closed. Otherwise you need to handle them carefully to keep the ingredients from spilling out.)

Heat about 1/2 inch of oil in a saucepan over high heat for 5 minutes, or until a tiny drop of water dropped into the pan sizzles immediately. (If you use a pan that is slightly larger around than one of the chimichangas you won't need as much oil. Use caution when testing the oil: too much water can cause the hot oil to splash violently.) Place a chimichanga in the pan, flap side down, and cook for 2 minutes on each side, or until lightly browned. Remove from the pan and drain on paper towels. Continue the process with the remaining chimichangas.

Place one chimichanga on each plate and serve with the salsa and sour cream.

TOMATOES FARCI (MEATBALL-STUFFED TOMATOES)

J: When I was little, I hated tomatoes in all forms except, of course, ketchup. As I've gotten older, they've grown on me. Tomatoes Farci sounds weird, but blame that on Megan. This is another dish she found in her travels in France. To me it's just little meatballs inside of tomatoes, and how can that be bad?

SERVES 4

4 large tomatoes

Salt and pepper

1/2 small onion

2 slices bread

1 egg

12 ounces ground beef

1/2 teaspoon Italian seasoning

2 1/4 cups water

1 cup rice

🏅 FOOD TRIVIA

The earliest recorded ground meat recipes are found in a book written by Marcus Gavius Apicius in ancient Rome. The section dedicated to recipes with ground meat includes this . . . ummm, interesting rating: "The ground meat patties of peacock have first place, if they are fried so that they remain tender. Those of pheasant have second place, those of rabbit third, those of chicken fourth, and those of suckling pig fifth." Can you imagine your friends' faces if you served them peacock meatballs?

Preheat the oven to 350°F.

Cut the tops off the tomatoes and scrape out the insides with a spoon. Season the insides with salt and pepper and place on a baking pan.

Peel the onion, chop into 1/8- to 1/4-inch pieces, and place in a large bowl. Tear the slices of bread into small pieces and add to the bowl along with the egg, ground beef, and Italian seasoning. Season with salt and pepper and mix with your hands until the ingredients are thoroughly combined. Roll the meat into 1-inch balls and place 5 or 6 inside each tomato. (You can just fill each tomato with the meat mixture, but they will take a lot longer to cook.) Bake for 35 to 40 minutes, until the meatballs are browned and firm to the touch.

Meanwhile, place the water in a saucepan and bring to a boil. Add the rice, cover, and cook over low heat for 20 minutes, or until most of the water is absorbed. Remove from the heat and let stand for 5 minutes, or until all of the water is absorbed.

To serve, place some of the rice on each plate and top with a stuffed tomato.

TRES LECHES CAKE

POTATO
CHORIZO
EMPANADAS

QUESO DIP WITH
TORTILLA CHIPS

SHRIMP
QUESADILLAS

MINI BLACK BEAN
TOSTADAS

CINCO DE MAYO

Contrary to popular opinion, Cinco de Mayo is not Mexican Independence Day. It is actually the day that the Mexican army, led by General Ignacio Zaragoza and helped by American troops, defeated Napoleon III's invading French army at the Battle of Puebla on May 5, 1862. Mexican Independence Day is when Mexico declared its independence from Spain on September 16, 1810.

Now that we have that straightened out, let's just say that it's a good excuse to have one more party before everyone heads home for the summer. Besides, Cinco de Mayo parties are always fun because the music is lively and they include lots of **wonderful, spicy food** that's easy to make.

SHRIMP QUESADILLAS

J: The combination of shrimp and green chiles is fantastic on these quesadillas. It doesn't matter what size shrimp you buy because you'll have to cut them up anyway, so save some money and buy the smallest frozen shrimp they have.

MAKES 36 PIECES

1 pound peeled and deveined cooked shrimp

2 (4-ounce) cans diced green chiles

4 cups shredded cheddar-Jack cheese

12 8-inch flour tortillas

Cut each shrimp into 1/2-inch pieces and place in a large bowl. Add the chiles and cheese and stir until evenly distributed.

Place a tortilla in a large sauté pan over medium-high heat and spread about 3/4 cup of the shrimp mixture over the tortilla. Top with another tortilla and cook for 2 minutes, or until the cheese begins to melt. Turn the quesadilla over and cook for 1 minute, or until the cheese is completely melted. Repeat the process with the remaining ingredients and cut each tortilla into 6 wedges. Place the wedges on a serving plate and serve warm.

MINI BLACK BEAN TOSTADAS

J: These mini tostadas are ideal because you get all the flavors in one bite. You can use any kind of chips, but the scoops that are shaped like little bowls hold everything together well.

MAKES ABOUT
40 TOSTADAS

Tortilla chips

1 (15-ounce) can black beans

1 cup chunky salsa or pico de gallo

1 cup shredded cheddar cheese

Arrange the tortilla chips in a single layer on a serving platter. Drain the beans and spoon a few of the beans on each chip. Top with a small spoonful of salsa and sprinkle with the cheddar cheese. (If your platter isn't large enough to hold them all, you can layer them.)

 BARGAIN SHOPPER

Cheese can be expensive, but it often goes on sale. I use a lot of shredded cheese so whenever it's on sale, I stock up and keep it in the freezer until I need it. You can save $4 to $6 per pound that way and it doesn't change the flavor at all. Besides that, you'll always have it when you need it.

QUESO DIP WITH TORTILLA CHIPS

J: This is the world's easiest dip to make and it's delicious. Even if you aren't having a Cinco de Mayo party, this is a great dip to make when you are just hanging out with friends.

MAKES ABOUT 2 CUPS

1 pound American cheese
1/2 cup chunky salsa
Tortilla chips

Cut the cheese into 1-inch cubes. Place the cheese and salsa in a small saucepan and cook over medium-low heat, stirring constantly, for 10 minutes, or until the cheese is melted. (Alternatively, if you have a microwave, place the cheese and salsa in a microwave-safe bowl. Cook on high heat for 2 minutes, stir, and continue to cook 1 minute at a time, stirring after each minute, until the cheese is completely melted.)

Place the queso dip in a bowl in the center of a large platter and arrange the chips around the bowl. (You will need to reheat this periodically by placing it back on the stove or in the microwave for 1 to 2 minutes.)

 FOOD TRIVIA

In 1912 a chemist named Wilbur Scoville devised a way to measure the heat of chile peppers. The basic idea is how much water needs to be added before you stop feeling the heat. Pepperoncinis rate 100 to 500 Scoville units; poblanos, 1,000 to 2,000; jalapeños, 2,500 to 8,000; cayennes, 30,000 to 50,000; habaneros, 100,000 to 325,000; and all the way at the top of the scale are red habaneros, at 350,000 to 577,000 units.

 PARTY STARTERS

Here are a couple of ideas to liven up your party.

HAVE A CHILE PEPPER EATING CONTEST.
You can be kind and use pepperoncinis, or you can really heat things up by using jalapeños. Just make sure you have plenty of beverages to put out the fire!

PLAY PIN THE TAIL ON THE DONKEY.
Okay, we probably sound like the world's biggest dorks, but trust us on this one. If you wait until later in the party, when your friends have loosened up a bit, this can be extremely amusing. Just make sure to use tape on the tails instead of thumbtacks because you never know where they're going to wind up.

POTATO CHORIZO EMPANADAS

J: These are a little more work than the other dishes for this party, but they are so yummy we couldn't skip them. They can be made several hours ahead and refrigerated, or they can be frozen for up to 2 months and baked at the last minute.

1 small potato

1/2 small onion

1/2 pound chorizo

4 prepared piecrusts

1 egg

Peel the potato and cut into 1/4-inch cubes. Peel the onion and cut into 1/4-inch pieces.

Place the potato, onion, and chorizo in a large sauté pan and cook over medium heat, stirring occasionally, for 15 minutes, or until the potatoes are cooked through. Drain on paper towels and let cool.

Preheat the oven to 375°F, if baking immediately.

Cut the dough into 3-inch circles with a cookie cutter. (A knife run around the outside of a glass also works well.) Spoon a teaspoonful of the chorizo mixture into the center of each dough circle. Dip your finger in water and wet the entire edge of the dough. Fold the dough over to form a half circle and press the edge firmly with a fork to seal. Arrange the empanadas on a baking sheet. Place the egg in a small bowl and beat until combined. Brush the egg over the empanadas and bake for 20 to 25 minutes, until golden brown. Place the empanadas on a large plate and serve warm.

SETTING THE SCENE

Although decorations aren't required, they do make it feel more like a celebration. You can decorate with brightly colored flowers made with tissue paper and pipe cleaners. (And you thought you'd never find a use for that skill you learned in grade school.) You can also usually find sombreros at party stores pretty inexpensively. A piñata is another fun decoration that doesn't cost much, but you may want to forgo breaking it open. Swinging a stick around while blindfolded can be hazardous to your walls, not to mention your guests.

If you don't want to have your friends deal with costumes, you can make tissue paper flowers for the girls to wear in their hair.

TRES LECHES CAKE

J: This traditional Mexican dessert is the most unusual cake I have ever made, but it's excellent. The cake rises when it bakes, falls when it cools, and rises again when it absorbs all of the milk topping. Serve it in small bowls because once it is cut, the liquid comes out to form a sauce.

SERVES 12

CAKE

4 eggs

1¹/₂ cups sugar

1 tablespoon baking powder

1¹/₂ cups flour

¹/₂ cup milk

TOPPING

1 cup milk

1 (12-ounce) can evaporated milk

1 (14-ounce) can sweetened condensed milk

16 ounces sour cream

To prepare the cake: Preheat the oven to 350°F. Lightly coat a 9 by 13-inch baking pan with butter or cooking spray.

Separate the eggs, placing the egg whites in a large bowl, reserving the yolks for later use. Beat the egg whites with a whisk or fork for 5 minutes, or until they remain upright when the whisk is pulled out. Gradually whisk in the sugar. Add the egg yolks and whisk until just combined. Add the baking powder. Alternate adding the flour and milk, stirring well after each addition. (Adding the flour and milk a little at a time helps keep the egg whites from deflating.) Pour the batter into the pan and bake for 40 to 45 minutes, until the cake springs back when lightly pressed in the center. Cool completely.

To prepare the topping: Place the topping ingredients in a large bowl and mix well. Pour over the cooled cake and refrigerate until ready to serve.

Cut the cake into squares and serve in small bowls.

♫♪ MUSIC

To make your Cinco de Mayo a bit more festive, simply play some Mexican music. Mariachi bands are popular at Cinco de Mayo festivals throughout Mexico and the United States. You can find fairly inexpensive CDs at your local music store, and of course, stores that sell secondhand CDs are even cheaper. I suppose you could always hire a mariachi band, but besides being expensive, neighbors tend not to appreciate mariachi bands blaring at midnight.

Dancing is always a good way to get people involved. Try learning a Mexican hat dance, or another traditional Mexican folk dance, such as the *Tlacoloreros* or *Cascada de Flores*, and teaching it to your friends.

EAT YOUR GREENS

Most college kids like the idea of eating healthy, but then find it easier to eat fast food than to make something that's healthier to eat. These salads are a **super simple and delicious** way to help you get in a few more vegetables. Each salad is substantial enough to serve four people as a meal or eight people as a side to a main dish. If the fact that they are easy and taste great isn't enough incentive for you, just think about your mom's reaction to the inevitable question, "Have you been eating right?" when you can answer, "I made a Tuscan salad for dinner last night." That falls into the priceless category.

ITALIAN TOMATO SALAD

J: The fresh basil and mozzarella give this salad such terrific fresh flavors that it's like a little bit of summer all year long. It's easy to put together, and it's light but also filling. If you're not a fan of green olives, use black olives or just leave them out. The salad will still be delicious.

SERVES 4

3 tomatoes

1 cucumber

2 green onions

8 ounces fresh mozzarella cheese

1/4 cup sliced green olives

1 tablespoon chopped fresh basil

1 tablespoon lemon juice

3 tablespoons olive oil

Salt and pepper

Cut the tomatoes in half and remove and discard the stems and seeds. Cut into 1-inch wedges and place in a large bowl.

Peel the cucumber, cut in half lengthwise, and remove and discard the seeds by running a spoon down the center. Cut each piece in half lengthwise again, slice into 1/4-inch-thick pieces, and add to the bowl.

Trim the green onions, discard the ends, and cut the white and about 1 inch of the green parts into thin slices and add to the bowl. Cut the mozzarella into 1/4-inch cubes and add to the bowl. Add the green olives to the bowl.

Place the basil and lemon juice in a small bowl and slowly add the olive oil, mixing briskly with a whisk or fork. Season with salt and pepper. Pour the vinaigrette over the salad and toss until combined. Serve immediately.

 FOOD TRIVIA

In 1893 the United States Supreme Court ruled that although botanically a tomato is a fruit, the Tariff Act in dispute could use the ordinary meaning of the words "fruit" and "vegetable," which classify a tomato as a vegetable. So technically this is a fruit salad, but legally it's a vegetable salad. But wait, what about the cucumbers? I guess we'll have to get that answer in their next session.

TUSCAN SALAD

M: This hearty salad is perfect as a meal. The cannellini beans, ham, and
eggs add a lot of substance, so this is no wimpy little bowl of greens.
The best part, though, is that it's so quick and easy to put together.

SERVES 4

2 eggs

1 (15-ounce) can cannellini beans

1/2 pound thick-sliced ham

2 tomatoes

2 green onions

1 head romaine lettuce

1 clove garlic

1 tablespoon white wine vinegar

3 tablespoons olive oil

Salt and pepper

 FOOD TRIVIA

Have you ever heard the saying, "living high on the hog"? It actually started back in the sixteenth century when the servants, slaves, and poor could only afford to eat pig's shoulder, feet, chitterlings, and cracklings, whereas the rich could afford the prime cuts of pork, which are found on the upper part of the hog. Since ham comes from the upper part that means college students live high on the hog. They may need to rethink that saying because that's just wrong.

Place the eggs in a small saucepan and cover with cold water. Bring to a boil and cook over medium-high heat for 5 minutes. Remove the pan from the heat and let stand until the water cools. Peel the eggs and cut into 1/4-inch-thick slices.

Drain the cannellini beans and place in a large bowl.

Cut the ham into 1/4-inch cubes and place in the bowl.

Cut the tomatoes in half and remove and discard the stems and seeds. Cut the halves into 1-inch wedges and place in the bowl.

Trim the green onions, discarding the ends, and cut all of the white and about 1 inch of the green parts into thin slices and add to the bowl.

Tear the romaine into bite-size pieces and add to the bowl.

Peel the garlic, finely chop, and place in a small bowl with the white wine vinegar. Slowly add the oil, mixing briskly with a whisk or fork. Season with salt and pepper. Pour the vinaigrette over the salad and toss until combined. Garnish with the egg slices and serve immediately.

WINTER SALAD

SERVES 4

J: Beets are another one of those things that sounded gross so I wouldn't try them. By now you know the next line . . . once I tried them I really liked them. They are sweeter than most vegetables, which is fine by me. This salad can be eaten as a side dish, but with the potatoes and eggs, it's filling enough to make a meal of it.

2 pounds small red potatoes

2 eggs

2 (15-ounce) cans whole beets

1 small onion

1 tablespoon chopped fresh parsley

2 teaspoons Dijon mustard

3 tablespoons canola oil

Salt and pepper

Place the potatoes in a large saucepan and cover with water. Cook over medium-high heat for 20 to 30 minutes, until a fork slides easily into the largest potato. Drain and let cool. Peel the potatoes and cut into 1/8- to 1/4-inch-thick slices.

While the potatoes are cooking, place the eggs in a small saucepan and cover with cold water. Bring to a boil and cook over medium-high heat for 5 minutes. Remove the pan from the heat and let stand until the water cools. Peel and cut each egg into 4 wedges.

Drain the beets and dice into 1/4-inch cubes. Peel the onion and chop into 1/4-inch pieces.

Place the parsley and mustard into a small bowl and slowly add the oil, mixing briskly with a whisk or fork. Season with salt and pepper.

Place the potatoes, beets, and onions in a large bowl. Pour the vinaigrette over the ingredients and toss until well combined. Season with salt and pepper, garnish with the egg wedges, and serve immediately. (If you are making this ahead of time, toss in the beets just prior to serving or the whole salad will turn red.)

 FOOD TRIVIA

Wild beets are believed to have originated in the Mediterranean area in prehistoric times. The ancients ate the greens, but used the root for medicinal purposes only. It was regarded as a laxative, a cure for bad breath, coughs, headaches, even as an aphrodisiac. It wasn't until the second or third centuries that the Romans first gave recipes for the root. I won't even comment on the fact that it took three thousand years to figure out beets were edible, but I will question how something can be a laxative and an aphrodisiac. I have trouble with that one.

SPINACH SALAD WITH STRAWBERRIES AND GOAT CHEESE

M: So you think you don't like goat cheese, huh? Well, have you ever tried it? This salad is a super tasty combination that is perfect for hot summer days when you don't want to make anything warm. And, if you're absolutely opposed to goat cheese, feta or blue cheese also works well.

SERVES 4

1 egg white

1/2 cup pecans

1 tablespoon plus 1 teaspoon sugar

1 pound strawberries

2 tablespoons white wine vinegar

1/4 cup canola oil

12 ounces baby spinach

1/2 cup crumbled dry goat cheese

🔆 FOOD FOR THOUGHT

Popeye knew what he was doing when he popped open that can of spinach. It's packed with the antioxidant beta-carotene and has strong, proven anticancer benefits. One and one-half cups of raw spinach contains 70 percent of the daily recommended amount of vitamin A, 25 percent of vitamin C, 20 percent of iron, 6 percent of calcium, 5 grams of fiber, and is only 40 calories. It sounds too good to be true . . . but it's not.

Preheat the oven to 375°F. Lightly coat a baking pan with oil or cooking spray.

Place the egg white in a small bowl, add the pecans, and toss until completely coated. Remove the pecans with a fork, draining off as much of the egg white as possible, and place on the baking pan. (You just want the pecans wet so the sugar will stick.) Sprinkle 1 tablespoon of the sugar over the pecans and toss lightly to coat evenly. Bake for 10 minutes, or until the pecans are dry.

Remove and discard the tops from the strawberries and cut each one into quarters. Place 1/2 cup of the strawberries into a small bowl and smash with a fork until they are in tiny pieces. Add the remaining 1 teaspoon sugar and the vinegar to the bowl and stir well. Slowly add the oil, mixing briskly with a whisk or fork.

Place the spinach, goat cheese, pecans, and remaining strawberries in a large bowl. Add the vinaigrette just prior to serving and toss until well combined. (The salad can be prepared ahead of time, but don't toss with the vinaigrette until you are ready to serve or the spinach will wilt.)

ANTIPASTO PASTA SALAD

J: You can serve this salad as a side dish, but it's so packed with stuff
that it can easily be a meal. I love this kind of dish because I can have
it as a meal one day and then snack on the leftovers for a few days
(right out of the container, of course).

8 ounces uncooked gemelli, penne, or bowtie pasta

1 red pepper

1/2 cup sun-dried tomatoes (packed in oil)

4 ounces fresh mozzarella cheese

1 (13-ounce) jar artichoke hearts

1 (3-ounce) can sliced black olives

1 clove garlic

2 tablespoons chopped fresh parsley

2 tablespoons lemon juice

1/4 cup olive oil

Salt and pepper

🏵 FOOD TRIVIA

Thomas Jefferson is credited with introducing macaroni to the United States. It seems that he fell in love with a dish he sampled in Naples while serving as the U.S. ambassador to France, and he promptly ordered crates of macaroni, along with a pasta-making machine, sent back to the States. All I have to say is, thanks, Tom!

Place a large saucepan of salted water over medium-high heat and bring to a boil. Add the pasta and cook for 10 to 12 minutes, until al dente. Drain in a colander and run under cold water for 1 to 2 minutes, until the pasta is thoroughly cooled. (This will also keep the pasta from sticking together.) Transfer the pasta to a large bowl.

Place the whole red pepper directly on the stove burner and turn to high heat. Cook the pepper for 3 or 4 minutes on each side, or until almost completely black. (If you have an electric stove, cook the pepper under the broiler instead of on the stovetop.) Place the pepper in a small bowl, cover tightly with plastic wrap, and let stand for 10 minutes. (The steam will make the skin peel right off.) Scrape the charred skin from the pepper, cut in half, and remove and discard the stem and seeds. Cut the halves into 1/4 by 1-inch strips and add to the bowl.

Drain the oil from the sun-dried tomatoes, cut into 1/8-inch strips, and add to the bowl. Cut the mozzarella into 1/4- to 1/2-inch cubes and add to the bowl. Drain the artichokes, cut into quarters, and add to the bowl. Drain the olives and add to the bowl.

Peel the garlic, finely chop, and place in a small bowl with the parsley and lemon juice. Slowly add the oil, mixing briskly with a whisk or fork. Season with salt and pepper. Pour the vinaigrette over the pasta and toss until combined. Cover with plastic wrap and refrigerate until ready to serve.

CUCUMBER MELON SALAD

M: This is another dish I swiped from the French. I was skeptical when I
first saw it, but the combination of the cantaloupe, cucumber, tomato,
and lime juice give it a fresh, clean flavor that is different from any
salad I had ever tried before. Prosciutto is a delicious, thin, smoky Italian cured ham. If you can't get it at your deli counter, get the smokiest
ham they have and ask them to slice it as thin as possible.

1 small cantaloupe

1 lime

2 cucumbers

2 tomatoes

4 slices prosciutto (optional)

2 tablespoons chopped fresh
chives

2 tablespoons white wine
vinegar

1/4 cup olive oil

Salt and pepper

1/4 cup sunflower seeds

Cut the melon in half and remove and discard the seeds. Cut
each half into 4 wedges and remove and discard the skin.
Cut each wedge widthwise into 1/4-inch-thick slices and place
in a large bowl. Cut the lime in half and squeeze the juice over
the cantaloupe.

Peel the cucumbers, cut in half lengthwise, and scrape out
the seeds with a spoon. Cut the cucumber into 1/8- to 1/4-inch-
thick slices and add to the bowl.

Cut the tomatoes in half and discard the stem and the
insides. Cut into 1/4-inch strips and add to the bowl.

Cut the prosciutto into 1/2 by 1-inch strips and add to
the bowl.

Place the chives and white wine vinegar in a small bowl
and slowly add the oil, mixing briskly with a whisk or fork.
Season with salt and pepper. Pour the vinaigrette over the
fruit and vegetables, add the sunflower seeds, and toss until
well combined. Cover with plastic wrap and refrigerate
until ready to serve.

 FOOD FOR THOUGHT

Cantaloupe is the most nutritious of all melons. It is naturally
sweet, low in calories and fat,
and packs a powerful nutri-
tional punch. It is rich in fiber
and carbohydrates, the nutrient
that fuels your brain and mus-
cles, and high in potassium, an
electrolyte that is responsible
for cell and muscle growth and
for maintaining normal fluid
balance. It is also loaded with
cancer-fighting beta-carotene
and is high in vitamin C.

BLUEBERRY SALAD WITH BRIE CROUTONS

J: The saying "The whole is greater than the sum of its parts" was written for this salad. It seems like a simple salad with very few ingredients, but something happens when they are all put together. I can't explain it so you'll have to trust me on this one. It is absolutely outstanding.

SERVES 4

1 crusty French bread roll (about 5 or 6 inches long)

2 ounces Brie cheese

2 tablespoons honey

2 tablespoons white wine vinegar

1/4 cup canola oil

Salt and pepper

6 ounces spring greens

1/2 pint blueberries (about 1 cup)

FOOD TRIVIA

A little blueberry trivia: Blueberries have more antioxidants than almost any other fruit or vegetable. One of nature's few blue foods, blueberries are one of the few berries native to North America. Blueberries were an important staple food of Native Americans. They dried and added them to any food that needed extra flavor and made a strong tea from their roots to use as a relaxant during childbirth.

Preheat the broiler to high heat.

Cut the bread into eight 1/2-inch-thick slices and spread some of the Brie on each slice. Arrange on a baking sheet and place under the broiler for 2 to 3 minutes, until the cheese is soft and the bread is light golden brown on the edges.

Combine the honey and vinegar in a small bowl and slowly add the oil, mixing briskly with a whisk or fork. Season with salt and pepper.

Place the salad greens and blueberries in a large bowl and add the vinaigrette. Toss until the salad is thoroughly coated.

Divide the salad between four bowls or plates and serve with the Brie croutons on the side.

ZUCCHINI OLIVE SALAD

M: Before I was an exchange student in France, I wasn't sure how I felt about raw zucchini. I now know how delicious it can be. Using a vegetable peeler to make long pasta-like strips for this yummy salad will give it a sophisticated look, but you can also simply grate or thinly slice them, so do whatever makes you happy.

SERVES 4

3 zucchini (about 1 1/2 pounds)

1 clove garlic

1 tablespoon chopped fresh basil

1/4 cup lemon juice

3 tablespoons olive oil

Salt and pepper

1/2 cup grated Parmesan cheese

1/2 cup sliced black olives

1/2 cup sunflower seeds

Peel the zucchini and discard the skin. Using a vegetable peeler, peel the zucchini into thin strips and place into a bowl.

Peel the garlic, finely chop, and place it in a small bowl. Stir in the basil and lemon juice. Slowly add the olive oil, mixing briskly with a whisk or fork. Season with salt and pepper.

Add the Parmesan cheese, black olives, and sunflower seeds to the zucchini. Just prior to serving, pour in the vinaigrette, toss until all the ingredients are coated, and season with salt and pepper.

FOOD TRIVIA

The exact origins of cheese making are unknown, but estimates range from around 8000 B.C., when sheep were domesticated, to around 3000 B.C. It was most likely discovered in Central Asia or the Middle East and spread to Europe, becoming a sophist-cated enterprise by Roman times. Parmesan cheese originated in Parma or in Tuscany in the eleventh century. Parmigiano-Reggiano is made only from April 1 to November 11, with milk from cows that have been grazing on fresh grasses.

CARAMELIZED BANANA CAKE

SAUTÉED VEGETABLES
ON CROSTINI

GARLIC
SHRIMP

TAPENADE

GOAT CHEESE-
STUFFED
MUSHROOMS

BEEF BROCHETTES
WITH HORSERADISH DIP

TAPAS PARTY

Initially, we were a bit nervous to put this into the book, especially when everyone thought we were saying "topless party," but with such incredible food and interesting history (see page 75), we just couldn't leave it out. Although they originated in Spain, tapas are so well suited to today's casual style that they have caught on in many areas of the world. The word originated as a name for the few **small bites of food** that were served with wine, but it has come to encompass almost any hot or cold food that can be served in small portions.

This party idea is a little more low-key than the others, but that doesn't mean that it can't be just as much fun. With food this delicious and a few good friends, you can't go wrong.

GARLIC SHRIMP

M: This easy and show-stopping dish has a little zip to it and will add life to the party. If you don't like spicy food, you can cut down on the red pepper. This tapa should be cooked at the last minute and served hot. The shrimp cook so fast that you can finish it in less than 5 minutes and it will fill your apartment with mouthwatering aromas.

MAKES 40 TO 50 PIECES

4 garlic cloves

1/4 cup olive oil

1 teaspoon red pepper flakes

1 pound medium, peeled and deveined raw shrimp

2 tablespoons lemon juice

Peel the garlic, finely chop, and place in a large sauté pan with the oil and red pepper flakes. Cook over medium-high heat for 30 seconds. Add the shrimp and lemon juice and cook, stirring constantly, for 3 to 4 minutes, until the shrimp turn pink and curl slightly. Place the shrimp on a plate and serve immediately with toothpicks on the side.

TAPENADE

M: Tapenade is essentially puréed olives with other flavorings added. This is a pretty mild version, but if you like the sharp taste of Kalamata olives, feel free to add more.

MAKES ABOUT 2 CUPS

1 (1-pound) French baguette loaf

1 clove garlic

1/4 cup olive oil

1/4 cup grated Parmesan cheese

1/4 teaspoon crushed red pepper

1 (5-ounce) can black olives

1/2 cup pitted Kalamata olives

Cut the bread into 1/4-inch-thick slices.

Peel the garlic and roughly chop. Place the garlic, olive oil, Parmesan cheese, and crushed red pepper into a blender and purée for 30 seconds, or until smooth. Drain the olives and add to the blender. Pulse for a few seconds at a time, until the olives are fairly finely chopped, but the mixture is not yet smooth. You will need to push the mixture down into the blender blades each time you stop the blender.

Serve in a bowl with a knife and the bread on the side.

BEEF BROCHETTES WITH HORSERADISH DIP

M: Normally, you would make these on skewers, but for a party it's much easier to broil all the meat and then serve them on toothpicks.

MAKES ABOUT
40 PIECES

6 shallots

1 tablespoon butter

2 pounds sirloin steak

Salt and pepper

1/2 cup mayonnaise

1 tablespoon horseradish

 FOOD TRIVIA

Tapas originated in the thirteenth century when, due to an illness, the Spanish king Alfonso X, had to take small bites of food with some wine between meals. Once recovered from the disease, the wise king decreed that no wine was to be served in any of the inns in the land of Castile, unless accompanied by something to eat. These little bites of food, originally just a slice of ham or a piece of cheese, also conveniently doubled as a cover for the glass or jar of wine to keep bugs or other impurities out of the drink. Eventually, they came to be called tapas, from the Spanish word *tapar* meaning to cover.

Peel the shallots and thinly slice into rings. Place in a small sauté pan with the butter and cook over medium-low heat, stirring occasionally, for 15 to 20 minutes, until the shallots are golden brown.

Adjust the oven rack to about 6 inches below the broiler element. Preheat the broiler to high. Lightly coat a broiler pan or baking sheet with cooking spray.

Cut the sirloin into 1-inch chunks and season with salt and pepper. Place the meat on the pan and broil for 4 to 5 minutes, until browned.

Place the mayonnaise and horseradish in a small bowl and stir until combined.

Arrange the meat on a serving platter, top each piece of meat with a few shallots, and insert a toothpick. Serve with the horseradish sauce on the side for dipping.

SAUTÉED VEGETABLES ON CROSTINI

M: This delicious dish can be prepared completely ahead of time. You can serve it at room temperature, but I like to reheat the vegetables before I serve them.

MAKES ABOUT
40 PIECES

1 (1-pound) French baguette loaf

1/4 cup olive oil

1 garlic clove

1 green pepper

1 red pepper

1 yellow pepper

1 pound fresh mushrooms

1 large red onion

Salt and pepper

Preheat the oven to 375°F.

Cut the baguette into 1/4- to 3/8-inch-thick slices and place them on a baking sheet. Brush the bread with 2 tablespoons of the olive oil. Bake for 7 to 9 minutes, until light brown and toasted. Peel the garlic and rub it over the warm bread slices.

Cut the peppers in half and remove and discard the stems and seeds. Slice the peppers into thin strips. Remove and discard the ends of the mushroom stems and thinly slice. Peel the onion, cut in half, and thinly slice.

Heat the remaining 2 tablespoons of olive oil in a large sauté pan and add the vegetables. (If all of the vegetables won't fit in your pan, cook what will fit for a few minutes until they cook down a little and then add the rest.) Cook over medium heat, stirring occasionally, for 20 minutes, or until all of the vegetables are soft. Turn the heat to high and cook for 5 more minutes, or until most of the liquid has been absorbed. Season with salt and pepper and serve in a bowl with a spoon and the crostini on the side.

♫♪ MUSIC

A good way to get your friends involved in your tapas party is to play traditional Spanish music. Flamenco or salsa music is always a hit. If you supply the castanets you'll have your friends dancing before you know it.

DRINKS

If you want to have a fun drink to serve with your tapas, you can make your own version of sangria. It is usually made with wine, but a mixture of fruit juices is just as good. Try peach with pineapple and orange juice or cranberry with raspberry and grape juice. Cut up fruit to float in it and serve it in festive glasses.

GOAT CHEESE–STUFFED MUSHROOMS

M: Even people who swear they don't like goat cheese love these. This delicious tapa is best eaten piping hot, so the mushrooms should be baked right before serving, but they can be made several hours ahead of time and refrigerated until you are ready to bake them.

MAKES ABOUT 32 MUSHROOMS

1 clove garlic

2 shallots

2 tablespoons olive oil

1/2 teaspoon Italian seasoning

5 ounces soft goat cheese

24 ounces fresh mushrooms

Preheat the oven to 425°F, if baking right away.

Peel the garlic and shallots and finely chop. Place the garlic and shallots in a small sauté pan with the oil and Italian seasoning. Cook over medium heat, stirring frequently, for 5 minutes, or until the shallots are soft. Remove from the heat and let cool. Add the goat cheese to the pan and stir until combined.

Remove and discard the mushroom stems and fill the cavities with the goat cheese mixture. Place the mushrooms on a baking sheet. (If you are preparing these in advance, cover with plastic wrap and refrigerate until ready to bake.) Bake for 15 minutes, or until the filling is bubbly. Place the mushrooms on a serving plate and serve immediately.

CARAMELIZED BANANA CAKE

M: Caramelized bananas are such a traditional tapas dessert that we had to find an easier way to serve them to a crowd. You've heard of pineapple upside-down cake. Well, why not try it with bananas?

SERVES 24

1/2 cup butter, softened

11/2 cups granulated sugar

3 eggs

2 teaspoons vanilla

1 cup milk

1 teaspoon salt

4 teaspoons baking powder

21/2 cups flour

1 cup firmly packed brown sugar

3 bananas

Preheat the oven to 350°F. Lightly coat a 9 by 13-inch baking pan with butter or cooking spray.

Place the butter and granulated sugar in a large bowl and stir until smooth. Add the eggs and stir for 2 minutes. Add the vanilla and milk and stir until combined. Add the salt, baking powder, and flour and stir until completely smooth.

Sprinkle the brown sugar evenly in the bottom of the pan. Cut the bananas into 1/4-inch-thick slices and arrange them over the brown sugar. Pour the batter over the bananas and bake for 35 to 40 minutes, until the center of the cake springs back when lightly pressed. Immediately place a cutting board or baking sheet over the cake and invert. Cool completely, cut into squares, and serve on small plates.

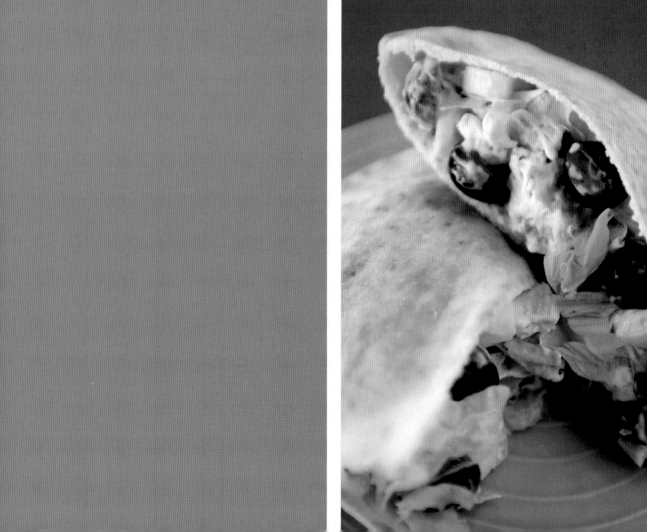

JUST LIKE MOM MAKES

Everyone knows that one of the best things about going home is having Mom cook all your favorite foods that you missed while you were away. Well, now you can learn to make them yourself. None of these are difficult to make and they all have that **home-cooked comfort-food** feel and taste. So, if you're feeling a little homesick, try one of these dishes—it's almost like being home. And hey, who knows, with a little practice you may even make it better than Mom does. (Although, you probably shouldn't tell her that.)

OVEN-BAKED CHICKEN PARMESAN

J: Chicken Parmesan is one of my favorite Italian dishes and my mom makes the best ever. It's the perfect combination of crunchy chicken and cheesiness, and because it's made in the oven, there's no oil mess on the stove. You may want to make extra because it's so good left over.

SERVES 4

1/4 cup flour

1 egg

1 cup cornflake crumbs

1 tablespoon water

4 boneless, skinless chicken breasts

1 (1 pound 10-ounce) jar prepared spaghetti sauce

1 cup shredded mozzarella cheese

1/4 cup Parmesan cheese

12 ounces uncooked spaghetti

VEG OUT

Eggplant Parmesan is just as sublime. Substitute an eggplant for the chicken, cut into 1/2-inch-thick slices, and follow the rest of the recipe.

Preheat the oven to 375°F. Lightly coat a baking pan with oil or cooking spray.

Place the flour, egg, and cornflake crumbs in separate shallow bowls. (If you don't have shallow bowls, use plates for the flour and cornflake crumbs.) Add the water to the bowl with the egg and beat well. Place the chicken breasts on a flat surface, cover with plastic wrap, and pound the thick parts with the bottom of a saucepan until they are about 1/2 inch thick. (If you are using thawed frozen chicken breasts that come in a big bag, they may be thin enough that they won't need to be pounded out.)

Dip the chicken breast completely in the flour to coat and shake off any excess. (Dipping in the flour first helps the egg and crumbs adhere.) Dip both sides of the chicken in the egg and then immediately place it in the cornflake crumbs, pressing slightly to make sure they stick. Place the chicken breast in the pan and repeat the process with the remaining chicken. Bake for 30 minutes, or until the chicken is done. (Insert a knife in the thickest part of one of the chicken breasts to make sure it is not pink.)

Place 2 tablespoons of the spaghetti sauce on top of each chicken breast and top with the mozzarella cheese. Sprinkle with the Parmesan cheese and bake for 8 to 10 minutes, until the cheese is melted.

Meanwhile, bring a large saucepan of salted water to a boil and add the spaghetti. Cook for 10 minutes, or until al dente. Drain the spaghetti in a colander and keep warm.

Heat the remaining spaghetti sauce in a small saucepan over medium-low heat.

Serve the chicken with the spaghetti and sauce on the side.

FOOD TRIVIA

The first American pasta factory was opened in Brooklyn, New York, in 1848, by a Frenchman named Antoine Zerega. He managed the entire operation with just one horse in his basement to power the machinery. To dry his spaghetti, he placed strands of the pasta on the roof to dry in the sunshine. Hmmm. A horse in the factory and drying pasta on the roof. I think the health inspectors might have a problem with it if you tried this today.

CHICKEN NOODLE SOUP

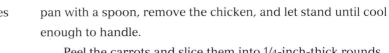

M: Homemade chicken soup is easy to make and tastes so much better than   SERVES 4
the stuff you get in a can that it's worth the extra time it takes. I use a
whole chicken to make the broth, but only put the dark meat in the soup.
You can use the white meat to make Chicken Salad Pitas or Barbecue
Chicken Pita Pizzas and save yourself the step of cooking the chicken.

1 whole chicken (3 to
4 pounds)

Salt and pepper

2 carrots

2 stalks celery

8 ounces uncooked noodles

1 teaspoon nutmeg

 FOOD FOR THOUGHT

If you refrigerate the chicken
broth after removing the
chicken, all of the fat will rise
to the top and harden. It can
then be easily removed to
make a soup that is virtually
fat-free.

Remove the assorted parts from inside the chicken and discard. Rinse the chicken well, place in a large stock pot, and
season with salt and pepper. Cover completely with water and
simmer over medium heat for 1 hour.

Skim off any impurities that have risen to the top of the
pan with a spoon, remove the chicken, and let stand until cool
enough to handle.

Peel the carrots and slice them into 1/4-inch-thick rounds.
Remove and discard both ends of the celery and cut into
1/4-inch-thick slices. Add the celery and carrots to the soup.

Remove the chicken from the bones, discarding the bones
and skin. Cut the dark meat into bite-size pieces, reserving the
white meat for another use. Add the chicken pieces, noodles,
and nutmeg to the pan, stir well, and season with salt and pepper. (Don't be surprised if you need to add a tablespoon or more
of salt. The soup will taste bland until you add enough salt.)
Cook, stirring occasionally, for 10 minutes, or until the noodles
are done. Remove from the heat and serve immediately.

CHICKEN SALAD PITA SANDWICHES

J: I love this chicken salad because it has fun stuff like grapes and celery in it. My mom always adds walnuts, but I say why ruin a good thing. You can cut some of the calories from this by using low-fat mayonnaise, but make sure to mix it in right before serving. Once it is mixed with the other ingredients, low-fat mayonnaise can get watery when it's refrigerated for a few hours.

SERVES 4

12 ounces boneless, skinless chicken

1 stalk celery

1/2 cucumber

1/2 cup grapes

1/4 cup mayonnaise

Salt and pepper

2 pieces pita bread

2 cups salad mix or shredded lettuce

 FOOD TRIVIA

The pocket in pita bread is made by steam. The steam puffs up the dough and, as the bread cools and flattens, a pocket is left in the middle. And here's a reason to learn to cook: legend has it that whoever eats the last piece of bread has to kiss the cook. That's the kind of story you only want to share with the right person.

Cut the chicken into 2-inch chunks and place in a small saucepan. Cover with water and cook over medium heat for 15 minutes, or until the chicken is cooked through. (Cut into one of the pieces to make sure there is no pink inside.) Remove from the heat, drain off the water, and cool completely.

Meanwhile, remove and discard both ends of the celery, cut in half lengthwise, and cut into 1/4-inch-thick pieces. Peel the cucumber, cut in quarters lengthwise, and cut into 1/4-inch-thick pieces.

Cut the chicken into bite-size pieces and place in a bowl. Cut the grapes in half and add to the bowl along with the celery, cucumber, and mayonnaise. Stir until well combined and season with salt and pepper.

To serve, cut the pita bread in half and open up the inside. Fill each piece with one quarter of the chicken salad and 1/2 cup lettuce.

PORK CHOPS WITH CARAMELIZED ONION MASHED POTATOES

J: Nothing says home to me more than pork chops and mashed potatoes. My mom always made these with the thick-cut boneless loin chops, but when I have to pay for them, it's the variety pack of thinner cut bone-in chops that always seem to be on sale. The good news is they cook faster and because of the gravy they don't get dried out.

SERVES 4

3 onions

2 tablespoons canola oil

2 pounds potatoes

1 teaspoon salt

2 pounds pork chops (4 to 6 chops)

Salt and pepper

2 teaspoons dried beef bouillon

3 tablespoons flour

1 1/2 cups water

3/4 cup milk

2 tablespoons butter

Peel the onions, cut them in half, and thinly slice. Place 1 tablespoon of the oil in a large frying pan over medium-high heat and add the onions. Cook, stirring occasionally, for 15 minutes, or until golden brown.

Meanwhile, peel the potatoes and cut into chunks. Place the potatoes in a saucepan, cover with cold water, and add the salt. Bring to a boil and then simmer over medium heat for 20 minutes, or until a fork slides easily into the potatoes.

While the potatoes are cooking, remove the onions from the pan and set aside. Add the remaining 1 tablespoon of oil to the pan and add the pork chops. Season the chops with salt and pepper and cook over medium-high heat for 2 to 3 minutes on each side, or until lightly browned. Place the beef bouillon and flour in a small bowl and slowly stir in the water a little at a time until all of the water is incorporated and the mixture is smooth. (If you put all the water in at once the flour will get lumpy and your gravy will never get smooth.) Add the mixture to the pan and stir well. Stir in half of the caramelized onions, cover, and cook over medium heat for 10 minutes.

Drain the potatoes and add the milk and butter to the pan. Cook over high heat for 2 to 3 minutes, until the milk comes to a boil. Remove the pan from the heat and mash the potatoes with a fork until fairly smooth. Stir in the remaining caramelized onions and season with salt and pepper.

Place a pork chop and some of the mashed potatoes on each plate and top with some of the gravy.

FOOD TRIVIA

Ever wonder why we call the government Uncle Sam? During the War of 1812, a New York pork packer named Uncle Sam Wilson shipped a boatload of several hundred barrels of pork to U.S. troops. Each barrel was stamped "U.S." on the docks, and it was quickly said that the "U.S." stood for "Uncle Sam," whose large shipment seemed to be enough to feed the entire army. Who would have thought the name came from pork.

FRESH TOMATO SOUP WITH
GRILLED CHEESE SANDWICHES

J: When I was little this was one of my favorite things to eat after a day of playing in the snow. After we moved to Arizona, my standards changed and now any day under 70 degrees works for me. Fresh tomato soup sounds like a pain, but, trust me, it's easy and well worth the effort.

SERVES 4

2 pounds ripe tomatoes

Salt

¼ teaspoon baking soda

2 cups milk

Pepper

2 tablespoons butter plus extra for sandwiches

8 slices bread

8 slices American cheese

Bring a saucepan of water to a boil and carefully drop in the tomatoes. Cook for 1 minute and drain off the water. (Blanching the tomatoes makes them a snap to peel.) Peel the tomatoes and remove and discard the stems. Place the tomatoes in the saucepan and squish them with your hands or smash them with a fork to break them into small pieces. Season with salt and cook over medium-low heat, stirring occasionally, for 15 minutes, or until the tomatoes are soft. Add the baking soda and stir well. Stir in the milk and 2 tablespoons butter and cook for 10 minutes, or until hot. Season with salt and pepper.

Heat a large sauté pan over medium-low heat. Butter one side of each of the bread slices and place 4 slices in the pan, buttered side down. Place 2 slices of cheese on each piece of bread and top with the remaining bread slices, buttered side up. Cook for 3 to 4 minutes on each side, until the cheese has melted and the bread is golden brown.

Place some of the soup in each bowl. Cut the grilled cheese in half and serve alongside the soup.

 FOOD TRIVIA

Although they are of American origin, tomatoes were unknown as food in this country until long after they were commonly eaten in Europe. We have Thomas Jefferson to thank for bringing them back to the United States when he started growing them at Monticello in 1781.

SALMON CAKES WITH POTATO WEDGES

J: I know this chapter is "Just Like Mom Makes," but this is actually one of my dad's specialties. With his culinary repertoire being limited to meatloaf, pot roast, salmon cakes, and any breakfast food, we were guaranteed to have these whenever Mom was out of town. Good thing we liked them. These are very similar to crab cakes, but since salmon is about one sixth of the cost of crabmeat we have them a lot more often.

SERVES 4

1½ pounds potatoes (about 5 potatoes)

3 tablespoons canola oil

Salt and pepper

1 (14-ounce) can salmon

4 cloves garlic

1 egg

1 tablespoon chopped cilantro

½ cup plus 1 tablespoon lemon juice

¾ cup breadcrumbs

½ cup mayonnaise

Preheat the oven to 400°F.

Cut each potato into 8 wedges and arrange on a baking sheet. Drizzle 1 tablespoon of the oil over the potatoes and toss until completely coated. Season with salt and bake for 30 minutes, or until lightly browned.

Meanwhile, drain the salmon and place in a large bowl. Finely chop 3 cloves of the garlic and add to the bowl. Add the egg, cilantro, ½ cup of the lemon juice, and the breadcrumbs and toss until combined. Form the mixture into 4 patties. Heat the remaining 2 tablespoons of the oil in a large sauté pan over medium-high heat and add the patties. Cook for 3 to 4 minutes on each side, or until golden brown.

Finely chop the remaining garlic clove and place in a small bowl. Add the mayonnaise and the remaining 1 tablespoon lemon juice, season with salt and pepper, and stir until combined.

Place a salmon cake on each plate, top with some of the mayonnaise, and serve hot with potato wedges on the side.

 BARGAIN SHOPPER

Although it is basically free to make breadcrumbs from old bread or buns that you were going to throw away anyway. I do it because I never seem to have breadcrumbs when I need them and I'm too lazy to go to the store. Simply dry the bread completely by either laying it out on a baking sheet for a couple of days or putting it in the oven at 200°F for about an hour. Then you can chop it up in the blender a little at a time until the crumbs are fairly fine. Or use the I-need-them-right-now method: toast the bread, let it cool completely, and then crumble it up into little pieces. For this recipe, the breadcrumbs can be a little chunky. Extra breadcrumbs can be stored in a resealable bag for several months.

BARGAIN SHOPPER

I love rice noodles in this recipe, but they can cost more than twice as much as regular pasta. If you can't get the rice noodles on sale, vermicelli is a fine substitute.

THAI CHICKEN

M: This is one of my absolute favorite recipes and it's so easy to make. The garlic gets the flavor going, the peanut butter adds the creaminess, and the chili paste adds the heat. I've said it before, but it bears repeating: if you haven't used chili paste before, be careful; it's extremely hot. You may want to start with one tablespoon and add more to taste.

SERVES 4

1 pound boneless, skinless chicken breasts

6 cloves garlic

1 teaspoon ground ginger

1/2 cup low-sodium soy sauce

2 tablespoons chili paste

1 onion

12 ounces rice noodles

1 tablespoon canola oil

1 tablespoon brown sugar

1/2 cup water

1/4 cup crunchy peanut butter

2 green onions

Cut the chicken into bite-size pieces and place in a bowl. Peel the garlic, finely chop, and add to the bowl. Add the ginger, soy sauce, and chili paste to the bowl and stir until well coated. Cover and refrigerate for 30 minutes.

Peel the onion, cut in half, and cut each half into 1/4-inch-thick slices.

Bring a large saucepan of salted water to a boil. Add the rice noodles and cook for 8 to 10 minutes, until al dente. Drain the noodles in a colander and keep warm.

Heat the oil in a large sauté pan over medium-high heat. Add the brown sugar and stir until dissolved. Add the onion and cook, stirring occasionally, for 5 minutes. Remove the chicken pieces from the marinade (but don't discard the marinade), add to the pan, and cook, stirring frequently, for 5 minutes. Add the marinade and water to the pan and bring to a boil. Reduce to low heat and cook for 5 minutes. Add the peanut butter, stir until completely incorporated, and remove from the heat.

Trim the green onions, discarding the ends, and cut the white and about 1 inch of the green parts into thin slices.

Toss the chicken with noodles, garnish with the green onions, and serve immediately.

 VEG OUT

Okay, this sounds like a complicated change, but it's not. Mix the marinade ingredients in a bowl, but don't marinate anything. Follow the rest of the directions, skipping the part about cooking the chicken, and add 2 cups of broccoli with the marinade. It's easy and delicious.

APPLE
STRUDEL

BEET
SALAD

BRATWURST

COLESLAW

GERMAN POTATO SALAD

OKTOBERFEST

Oktoberfest first began as a celebration of the marriage of Crown Prince Ludwig and Princess Therese on October 12, 1810. The citizens of Munich were invited to attend the festivities held on the fields in front of the city gates to celebrate the royal event. Horse races marked the close of the event and the decision to repeat the horse races in subsequent years gave rise to the tradition of Oktoberfest. In the almost two hundred years since then, it has evolved into one of the world's largest parties.

You don't need to plan anything on quite that grand a scale, but Oktoberfest is a good excuse to **get together with friends**. This party works either as a small gathering of close friends to enjoy some fine company and great food or as a larger party to celebrate the season. We've included a few ideas to help you get started, but think of them as just that, a starting point. We all know what Oktoberfest is really about, but with our mom watching we decided to only give suggestions for food.

BRATWURST

M: Nothing says German more than sausage, which makes bratwurst a must for any Oktoberfest celebration. This version is made with caramelized onions that get nice and sweet to make the perfect topping for the bratwurst.

SERVES 10 TO 12

2 onions

2 tablespoons butter

3 pounds bratwurst

15 to 18 hard rolls

Peel the onion and cut into 1/4-inch-thick slices. Break them apart and place them in a large frying pan with the butter. Cook over medium heat for 10 minutes, or until the onions begin to soften. Remove the onions from the pan and add the bratwurst. Cook over medium-high heat for 5 minutes, or until browned. Turn the bratwurst over and cook for 5 minutes, or until browned. (You will need to brown the bratwurst in 2 batches, but once they are all browned you can form 2 layers in the pan.) Add the onions and about 1/2 inch of water to the pan, cover, and cook over medium-low heat for 20 minutes. Remove the cover from the pan and cook over medium-high heat for 5 minutes, or until all of the liquid is cooked off.

Place a bratwurst on each roll and top with some of the onions. Serve immediately with spicy mustard on the side.

COLESLAW

M: I love this coleslaw and, of course, any German meal has to include cabbage of some sort. I like to make it with cider vinegar because it's a little sweeter, but my dad likes it made with white wine vinegar so it's a little tangier. Use whichever suits your taste.

SERVES 10 TO 12

1 cup mayonnaise

3 tablespoons cider vinegar

1/2 cup sugar

1 (16-ounce) package coleslaw mix

1/2 cup golden raisins

Combine the mayonnaise, cider vinegar, and sugar in a small bowl.

Place the coleslaw mix and raisins in a large bowl. Add the mayonnaise mixture and stir until completely coated. Cover with plastic wrap and refrigerate until ready to serve.

GERMAN POTATO SALAD

M: I'm not sure why this is called German potato salad. When we made it
for my German host family, they enjoyed the sweet-sour flavor, but
they had never had anything like it before. Oh well, it's good and it goes
great with the bratwurst. To save time during the party, this can be
made ahead and reheated on the stovetop or in the microwave just
before serving.

SERVE 10 TO 12

5 pounds red potatoes

1 pound bacon

1 onion

1/4 cup flour

1/3 cup white wine vinegar

1/3 cup sugar

3 cups water

Salt and pepper

Place the potatoes in a large pot and cover with cold water. Bring to a boil and cook over medium-high heat for 30 minutes, or until a fork slides easily into the largest potato. Drain off the water and let stand until cool enough to handle. Peel the potatoes and cut them into 1/8-inch-thick slices.

Cut the bacon strips into 1/4-inch-wide pieces, place in a large frying pan, and cook over medium heat for 10 minutes. Meanwhile, peel the onion and chop into 1/4- to 1/2-inch pieces. Add the onion to the pan and cook for 10 minutes, or until the bacon just begins to get crisp.

Remove the bacon and onions from the pan and drain on paper towels. Drain off most of the grease, leaving about 1/4 cup in the pan. Stir in the flour and cook over medium heat, stirring constantly, for 1 minute, or until it begins to bubble. Stir in the white wine vinegar and sugar. Slowly add the water, a little at a time, stirring until completely smooth after each addition. Cook for 5 minutes, or until the mixture is bubbly. Add the bacon and onion to the pan and stir until combined. Add the potato slices and stir gently until completely coated. (If your pan is too small to hold all the potatoes, you can pour the sauce over the potatoes in the bowl and stir.) Place in a serving bowl and serve warm.

BEET SALAD

M: Beets are a highly underused vegetable in the United States. In Europe you can buy whole cooked beets in any grocery store, but since here you have to buy them raw and cook them, I opt for canned beets to make this simple salad.

SERVES 10 TO 12

3 (15-ounce) cans sliced beets

1/2 small onion

1 tablespoon sugar

2 tablespoons white wine vinegar

Drain the beets. Peel the onion and cut into 1/8-inch-thick slices.

Combine the sugar and white wine vinegar in a bowl and let stand for 5 minutes, or until the sugar is dissolved. Add the beets and onions and toss until completely coated. Cover with plastic wrap and refrigerate until ready to serve.

 PARTY STARTERS

Here is a way to use Oktoberfest trivia at your party. You can give a prize for the person who guesses the closest.

Last year Munich's Oktoberfest boasted 6.3 million visitors. How many of each of the following items were consumed?

Pieces of chicken (487,000)

Pork sausages (380,000)

Pounds of fish (108,000)

Pork knuckles (56,000)

Bottles of water (721,000)

Gallons of beer (1,645,000)

How about a true or false test? We give you the true ones and you can have fun making up a bunch of false ones. Make some of them believable, like 38 Tyrolean hats or 23 wallets, and make some more outrageous like 4 pairs of fishnet stockings or 2 toupees. (Although it will be hard to top 3 pairs of dentures.) It will be fun to see if you can get your friends to fall for the ones you make up.

Which of the following items were actually in the 2005 Munich Oktoberfest lost and found?

550 IDs and credit cards

420 sets of keys

260 pairs of glasses

190 cell phones

85 children

3 pairs of dentures

APPLE STRUDEL

M: Making strudel dough from scratch is a pain, but puff pastry is a terrific substitute that makes this dessert surprisingly easy to put together. The crust gets all flaky, and with the apples and cinnamon . . . oh man, it's good.

SERVES 12

6 Granny Smith apples

1 tablespoon lemon juice

1 cup raisins

1 cup sugar plus extra for dusting

1 teaspoon cinnamon

2 tablespoons cornstarch

2 sheets puff pastry, thawed

1 egg yolk

Preheat the oven to 375°F. Line a baking sheet with parchment paper or aluminum foil and lightly coat with oil or cooking spray.

Peel and core the apples and cut into 1/8-inch-thick slices. Place them in a large bowl and toss with the lemon juice. Add the raisins, 1 cup sugar, cinnamon, and cornstarch and toss until combined.

Lay the sheets of puff pastry on a flat surface and spread half of the apple mixture down the center of each sheet. Fold the sides over the filling and transfer the strudels to the baking sheet, seam side down. Lightly beat the egg yolk, brush over the dough, and sprinkle lightly with sugar. Cut 5 evenly spaced slits across the top of the dough and bake for 30 to 40 minutes, until golden brown. Cool slightly and cut each strudel into 6 slices.

♫♪ MUSIC

When Germans celebrate, they love to sing and dance, so no Oktoberfest would be complete without a little German music. I think it's almost mandatory to have an oompah band playing in the background and, of course, the natural progression would be a dance contest. Germans are always associated with polkas so that's a fine place to start. Germans also love *Die Ente Tanz*, which literally translated means the duck dance. Yep, you guessed it, it's the chicken dance. Don't bother awarding a prize for the best dancer, stick with the sillier stuff like worst dancer, most energetic, best waddle, or the dancer most likely to cause bodily harm to others.

FOOD FOR THE MASSES

These dishes are for when you want to **feed a crowd** without breaking the bank or spending three days in the kitchen. All the recipes can be made ahead of time and either reheated or baked right before serving, so you don't need to spend any time in the kitchen while your friends are there. They are perfect no matter whether you want to have everyone over after a game or if you just want to have a bunch of friends come over to hang out.

RATATOUILLE WITH ITALIAN SAUSAGE

M: Ratatouille (ra-ta-TOO-ee) is a popular dish from the Provence region in France. It's a super simple vegetable-filled dish that makes enough to feed you, your roommates, and anyone else that smells it cooking. With tons of fresh veggies, this recipe is way healthier than anything you'd get at a fast food restaurant, and it's so easy to make.

3 zucchini (about 1½ pounds)

3 summer squash (about 1½ pounds)

1 onion

1 red bell pepper

1 yellow bell pepper

1 large eggplant

2 pounds Italian sausage

3 (14-ounce) cans crushed tomatoes

1 teaspoon Italian seasoning

Salt and pepper

Trim and discard the stems from the zucchini and summer squash and slice them into ¼-inch-thick rounds.

Peel the onion and dice into ¼- to ½-inch pieces. Cut the peppers in half, remove and discard the stems and seeds, and cut into ½-inch pieces. Remove and discard the stem from the eggplant and cut into ¾-inch chunks.

Cut the Italian sausage into ¼- to ⅜-inch-thick slices and place in a large stock pot. Cook over medium-high heat, stirring occasionally, for 5 minutes, or until browned. Add the zucchini, squash, onion, and peppers and cook, stirring occasionally, for 20 minutes, or until the vegetables start to soften. Add the eggplant and cook for 10 minutes, or until the vegetables are almost tender. Stir in the tomatoes and Italian seasoning, season with salt and pepper, and cook for 10 minutes, or until all of the vegetables are cooked through. Serve warm.

 FOOD TRIVIA

Everyone has their own version of how to cut an onion without crying. I'm not convinced that any of them work, but the most popular versions seem to be: 1) freeze the onions for half an hour before chopping; 2) peel them under running water; 3) don't slice the onion root, which releases the strongest fumes; 4) breathe through your nose while chopping. And we can't forget to include holding a piece of bread in your mouth as you chop, although I suggest you try this one when no one else is around.

 VEG OUT

Do I even have to say you can leave out the Italian sausage?

CHICKEN CACCIATORE

J: Cacciatore is an Italian word that refers to the rustic cooking style, where the meat is cooked right along with the vegetables. This is a cheap, easy, and incredibly tasty way to feed a lot of people. The chicken can be made completely ahead of time and heated up just prior to serving. Then all you have to do is cook the spaghetti, heat up a loaf of crusty bread, and you are good to go.

SERVES 10 TO 12

2 onions

1 pound fresh mushrooms

2 red peppers

2 cloves garlic

2 pounds boneless, skinless chicken breasts

1 tablespoon canola oil

5 (14-ounce) cans diced tomatoes

Salt and pepper

2 pounds uncooked spaghetti

Parmesan cheese

💡 FOOD FOR THOUGHT

This dish is traditionally made with whole chicken pieces that are braised, or cooked slowly, for several hours. By using cut-up chicken breasts, it not only decreases the cooking time substantially, it also cuts out a lot of the calories.

Peel the onions, cut in half, and thinly slice. Remove and discard the ends of the mushroom stems and thinly slice. Cut the peppers in half, remove and discard the stem and seeds, and cut into 1/2-inch pieces. Peel the garlic and finely chop. Cut the chicken into 1-inch pieces.

Place the oil, onions, mushrooms, and peppers in a large pot over medium-high heat and cook, stirring frequently, for 10 minutes. Add the chicken and cook, stirring frequently, for 10 minutes, or until the chicken is browned. Add the garlic and stir well. Drain the tomatoes and add to the pan. Season with salt and pepper and cook over low heat for 15 minutes, or until the onions and peppers are soft.

Meanwhile, bring a stock pot of salted water to a boil and add the spaghetti. Cook over medium-high heat for 10 minutes, or until al dente. Drain the spaghetti in a colander and keep warm.

Place some of the spaghetti in the center of each plate, spoon some of the chicken cacciatore on top, and sprinkle with the Parmesan cheese.

CHILI WITH GREEN CHILE CORNBREAD

J: My mom calls this chili, but my dad insists it's Mexican spaghetti. I don't care what they call it; anything that's super simple, delicious, and makes a lot is a winner in my book. As an added bonus, the ingredients are cheap and it can be made up to a day ahead and reheated. The green chile cornbread goes perfectly with the chili, but if you prefer you can leave out the chiles or heat it up with a finely diced jalapeño.

SERVES 10 TO 12

GREEN CHILE CORNBREAD

3 cups milk

4 eggs

2/3 cup canola oil

1/3 cup butter, melted

3 cups flour

2/3 cup sugar plus extra for dusting

1 cup cornmeal

2 tablespoons baking powder

1 teaspoon salt

1 (4-ounce) can diced green chiles

CHILI

1 onion

1 1/2 pounds ground beef

2 (15-ounce) cans kidney beans

3 (14-ounce) cans diced tomatoes

1/3 cup chili powder

3 cups water

8 ounces uncooked macaroni noodles

Salt and pepper

To prepare the cornbread: Preheat the oven to 350°F. Lightly butter or spray a 9 by 13-inch baking pan.

Combine the milk, eggs, oil, and melted butter in a large bowl. Add the flour, sugar, cornmeal, baking powder, and salt and stir until just combined. Drain the green chiles and stir into the batter. Pour the batter into the pan and sprinkle a light dusting of sugar over the top. Bake the cornbread for 40 to 50 minutes, until a toothpick inserted in the center comes out clean.

To prepare the chili: Peel the onion and dice into 1/2-inch pieces. Place the onion and ground beef in a large stockpot and cook over medium heat, stirring occasionally, for 15 minutes, or until the ground beef is browned. Drain the fat off the meat, washing the grease down the sink with hot running water. Add the kidney beans and tomatoes (do not drain them) and stir until combined. Stir in the chili powder and water and cook over medium heat for 10 minutes, or until it comes to a boil. Add the macaroni and cook for 10 minutes, or until the macaroni is soft. Season with salt and pepper and additional chili powder, if desired. (If you reheat the chili you may need to add a little water to keep it from sticking to the bottom of the pan.)

Spoon some of the chili into each bowl and serve with the cornbread on the side.

JAMBALAYA

M: I fell in love with this dish the first time I tried it in New Orleans. The combination of rice, tomatoes, shrimp, chicken, and andouille sausage is the epitome of Cajun cooking. This version isn't particularly spicy, so make sure to serve it with some hot sauce on the side for more adventurous eaters.

SERVES 10 TO 12

1 large onion

1 green pepper

3 stalks celery

4 cloves garlic

1 pound andouille or smoked sausage

1 pound boneless, skinless chicken breasts

2 tablespoons Cajun seasoning

2 (14-ounce) cans diced tomatoes

3 tablespoons dried chicken bouillon

8 cups water

4 cups rice

1 pound peeled and deveined raw shrimp

Peel the onion and chop into 1/2-inch pieces. Cut the green pepper in half, remove and discard the stems and seeds, and cut into 1/4- to 3/8-inch pieces. Remove and discard both ends from the celery stalks, cut the stalks in half lengthwise, and slice into 1/4-inch-thick pieces. Peel the garlic and finely chop.

Cut the sausage into 1/4-inch-thick rounds and place in a large stock pot. Cut the chicken into bite-size pieces, add to the pot, and cook over medium-high heat, stirring frequently, for 10 minutes, or until browned. Drain off any fat and add the onion, green pepper, celery, and garlic to the pot. Cook over medium heat, stirring frequently, for 10 minutes, or until the onions are soft. Add the Cajun seasoning, tomatoes, and chicken bouillon and stir well. Add the water and rice and stir well. Cover and cook over medium-low heat for 40 minutes, or until the rice is tender. Stir in the shrimp and let cook for 2 or 3 minutes, until the shrimp are pink.

Spoon the jambalaya into bowls and serve.

FOOD TRIVIA

Any good Louisianan will tell you, Cajun and Creole cooking are not the same. Cajun is the country cooking of Louisiana, highlighted by dirty rice, jambalaya, andouille sausage, and simple foods such as fried catfish. Putting more emphasis on butter and cream, Creole is the food of the city, a more refined cuisine represented by oysters Rockefeller, shrimp rémoulade, and bananas Foster. But, both Cajun and Creole use the "holy trinity" of New Orleans cooking: green peppers, onions, and celery. All I know is Cajun or Creole, it's all good eating.

LASAGNA

SERVES 10 TO 12

J: Lasagna is one of those dishes that sounds difficult even though it's not.
This version is particularly easy to put together because we use no-boil
noodles (which are a little thinner than the normal kind) and jarred sauce,
and it's still excellent. If you like your lasagna a little spicier, you can use
hot Italian sausage. Just serve this with some warm bread and you're there.

1 onion

2 cloves garlic

1 pound ground beef

Salt and pepper

1 (1 pound 10-ounce) jar
prepared spaghetti sauce

1 (9-ounce) box no-boil
lasagna noodles

32 ounces ricotta cheese

1 pound shredded
mozzarella cheese

Peel the onion and chop into 1/4-inch pieces. Peel the garlic
and finely chop.

Place the ground beef in a large sauté pan with the onions
and cook over medium-high heat, stirring frequently, for
10 to 12 minutes, until cooked through. Drain off any fat,
season with salt and pepper, and add the garlic to the pan.
Cook, stirring constantly, for 1 minute. Remove the pan from
the heat and stir in the spaghetti sauce.

Preheat the oven to 350°F.

Spread a little of the sauce around the bottom of a 9 by
13-inch baking pan. Arrange 4 noodles down the center of the
pan. (They won't go all the way to the sides of the pan, but they
will expand as they cook and fill in the edges.) Spread one third
of the sauce over the noodles and top with half of the ricotta
cheese and half of the mozzarella cheese. Continue the layering
with noodles, another third of the sauce, the rest of the ricotta,
more noodles, and cover with the remaining sauce. Cover the
pan tightly with aluminum foil. (The lasagna can be refrigerated
for up to 1 day before baking.) Bake for 1 hour. Remove the aluminum foil, sprinkle with the remaining mozzarella cheese, and
bake for 10 minutes, or until the cheese is bubbly. Remove from
the oven and let stand for 15 minutes before serving.

Cut into 12 squares and serve warm.

VEG OUT

This is an easy recipe to adjust
for vegetarians. You can just
leave out the meat, substitute
zucchini for the ground beef, or
add layers of spinach over the
sauce. There are many more
variations, but you get the idea.

🔖 FOOD TRIVIA

The origins of the word *lasagna*
are amusing and slightly dis-
gusting. First, the Romans bor-
rowed the Greek word *lasanon*
as a way to humorously refer to
a kind of pot to cook with. It
later became the Italian word
lasagne and came to refer to
a dish cooked in such a pot.
Soon, the word *lasagna* was
applied to the pasta itself. So
what's funny about that? The
original Greek word meant
chamber pot. I wouldn't share
that with your guests while
they are eating.

FOOD FOR THOUGHT

Couscous is a coarsely ground semolina pasta that is a staple in many North African countries. It started appearing on American dinner tables about ten years ago and is swiftly gaining in popularity not only because of its taste, but because it is loaded with complex carbohydrates, vitamin B, and minerals. This delicious, healthy meal is low in calories and each serving contains only 6 grams of fat and 1 gram of saturated fat. It also has 32 grams of protein and almost 7 grams of fiber. Your friends don't need to know that; they'll just know it's yummy.

MOROCCAN CHICKEN STEW WITH COUSCOUS

M: Jill and I fell in love with Moroccan food while we were studying in France and had to include a dish with those amazing flavors. The cinnamon, curry, and raisins that are commonly found in Moroccan cooking combine to give this stew an unexpected depth. When all the flavors are cooked together and served over the couscous it's sure to be a crowd-pleaser.

SERVES 8 TO 10

2 large red onions

2 green peppers

4 cloves garlic

2 tablespoons olive oil

2 teaspoons curry powder

1/2 teaspoon cinnamon

2 teaspoons salt

1 teaspoon pepper

2 teaspoons dried chicken bouillon

2 cups water

4 (14-ounce) cans diced tomatoes

2 pounds boneless, skinless chicken breasts

1 (5-ounce) can black olives

1 cup raisins

2 tablespoons lemon juice

1/4 cup chopped parsley

4 cups couscous

Peel the onions and cut into 1/4- to 1/2-inch pieces. Cut the peppers in half, remove and discard the stem and seeds, and cut into 1/4- to 1/2-inch pieces. Peel the garlic and finely chop.

Heat the oil in a large stock pot over medium-high heat. Add the onion and peppers and cook, stirring occasionally, for 5 minutes. Add the garlic, curry powder, cinnamon, salt, and pepper and cook for 1 minute, or until fragrant. Add the chicken bouillon, water, and tomatoes (with the juice) and bring to a boil. Reduce to medium heat, cover, and cook for 10 minutes.

Cut the chicken into bite-size pieces. Cut the olives in half. Add the chicken, olives, and raisins to the pot, cover, and cook for 8 to 10 minutes, until the chicken is cooked through. (Cut into one of the pieces to make sure there is no pink inside.) Remove the pot from the heat and stir in the lemon juice and parsley.

Meanwhile, bring 4 cups of water to a boil. Stir in the couscous and remove from the heat. Cover and let stand for 10 minutes, or until all of the water is absorbed. Fluff the couscous with a fork before serving.

Spoon some of the couscous in the center of each plate or shallow bowl and top with some of the stew.

IMPRESSING YOUR DATE

As much as we hate the saying, "the way to a man's heart is through his stomach," there is some truth to it. Guys like to have girls cook for them. But, here's a tip for you guys: girls find it just as appealing to have a guy cook for them. Anyone can take you out to eat, but making a nice dinner for someone shows that you care enough to put in the extra effort. You get bonus points for that.

We wrote these recipes a little bit differently than those in the other chapters. We've tried to make it as easy as possible for you to serve a nice dinner and make it look like you do it all the time. The directions include what to prepare ahead of time and then when to start each step so that everything will be finished at the same time. None of these meals is difficult. Just follow the directions step by step and your date is certain to be impressed.

GLAZED PORK TENDERLOIN WITH BAKED APPLES AND SWEET POTATOES

J: This is a superb date dish because all of the prep can be done and the mess cleaned up long before your date arrives. Then just bake and serve. We use pork tenderloin because it is all dark meat and it stays moist even if it's a little overcooked. With this classic combination of pork, apples, and sweet potatoes, even the most inexperienced cook can look like a pro.

SERVES 2

3 large gala or Fuji apples

1 pork tenderloin (about 1 pound)

Salt and pepper

1/2 cup apricot preserves or peach jam

1/4 cup brown sugar

1/2 teaspoon cinnamon

2 tablespoons raisins

1/4 cup butter, softened

1/4 cup confectioners' sugar

2 sweet potatoes

Up to 8 hours before mealtime, cut one of the apples into 8 wedges and arrange them down the center of a baking pan large enough to hold the tenderloin. (You don't serve these apples, they just add a little flavor and raise the tenderloin off the pan so it cooks evenly.) Heat a large sauté pan over medium-high heat, add the pork tenderloin, and cook for 2 to 3 minutes on each side, or until browned. Place the browned tenderloin on top of the apples, season lightly with salt and pepper, and spread the preserves over the top. Cover with plastic wrap and refrigerate until ready to bake.

Remove the cores from the remaining two apples by inserting a small knife near the core of each apple and cutting completely around the core. (The idea is to remove the core, keeping the apple whole, and creating a hole in the center of each apple.) Check inside the apples and remove and discard any remaining bits of the core. Combine the brown sugar, 1/4 teaspoon of the cinnamon, and the raisins in a small bowl and press half of the mixture firmly into the center of each apple. Place the apples in a baking pan, cover with plastic wrap, and set aside until ready to cook.

Stir the butter, confectioners' sugar, and the remaining 1/4 teaspoon of cinnamon together in a small bowl and refrigerate until ready to serve.

One hour and 15 minutes before mealtime, preheat the oven to 350°F.

One hour before mealtime, poke the sweet potatoes with a fork and arrange on a baking pan or a piece of aluminum foil and place on the lower rack in the oven. Remove the plastic wrap from the apples and place the baking pan on the lower rack of the oven next to the potatoes.

Fifty minutes before mealtime, remove the plastic wrap from the tenderloin and bake for 40 minutes, or until the meat is not pink. (Insert a knife in the center to check. The juices may still be a little pink, but the meat should be brown.

FOOD TRIVIA

Archeologists have found remains of apples in excavations of sites dating back to 6500 B.C. From the beginning they have been associated with love, beauty, luck, health, comfort, pleasure, wisdom, temptation, sensuality, sexuality, virility, and fertility. Is it any wonder that they have become the most popular fruit on earth? Just be careful not to throw them around. In ancient Greece, if a man tossed an apple to a girl, it was a proposal of marriage, and catching it signified acceptance.

If you are in doubt, put it back in the oven for 10 more minutes.)

Remove the tenderloin from the oven, cover with aluminum foil, and let rest for 10 minutes. Remove the potatoes from the oven and squeeze gently to make sure they are soft. If they are still firm, return them to the oven for 10 more minutes. Remove the apples from the oven and set aside. Slice the thin ends off the tenderloin and discard, then cut the remainder into 1/4-inch-thick slices.

Arrange 4 or 5 slices of the hot tenderloin on one side of each plate. Place one sweet potato on each plate, slice them open, and spoon some of the cinnamon-butter inside. Place a baked apple on each plate and spoon any sugar from the pan over the apples. Serve immediately.

ROASTED CHICKEN WITH PARSLEY POTATOES AND ASPARAGUS

J: I know that a 4-pound chicken is more than you need for two people, but if the point is to impress your date, you don't want to serve a scrawny little chicken. This dinner is delicious and easy to prepare, so if you are a novice, this is a fine place to start. Working with a whole chicken for the first time can be an intimidating experience, but actually there's nothing to it. The fresh parsley and rosemary turn these all-time favorite standards—chicken and potatoes—into a sophisticated dinner.

SERVES 2

PARSLEY POTATOES

1 bunch fresh parsley

1 pound small red potatoes

2 tablespoons lemon juice

1/4 cup butter, melted

Salt and pepper

ROASTED CHICKEN

1 whole chicken (about 4 pounds)

1 (2/3-ounce) package fresh rosemary

ASPARAGUS

1/2 pound asparagus

To prepare the potatoes: *Up to 3 hours before mealtime,* finely chop 2 tablespoons of the parsley. Cut the potatoes in half (or quarters, if they are large) and place on a baking pan. Drizzle the lemon juice and half of the melted butter over the potatoes and toss until evenly coated. Season with salt and pepper and sprinkle with the chopped parsley. Cover with plastic wrap, and set aside until ready to cook.

To prepare the chicken: *Up to 3 hours before mealtime,* reach inside the chicken cavity and remove the assorted parts and discard. (Often the innards are packed in a small package and placed inside the main cavity. Sometimes these are placed in the neck cavity, so be sure to check there, too.) Rinse the chicken well and pat dry. Cut off any visible fat around the cavities. Place the chicken in a baking pan with the breast side facing up. Remove the large stems from the remaining parsley and place the leaves in the cavity with the rosemary sprigs. Brush the outside of the chicken with a little of the remaining butter and sprinkle with salt and pepper. Cover with plastic wrap and refrigerate until ready to cook.

To prepare the asparagus: Break off the ends of the asparagus, place in a saucepan, and add about 1/2 inch of water. (Alternatively, if you have a microwave, place on a microwave-safe serving plate or shallow bowl. Add a few tablespoons of water and cover with waxed paper or plastic wrap.) Refrigerate until ready to cook.

One and one-half hours before mealtime, preheat the oven to 350°F.

One hour and 15 minutes before mealtime, remove the plastic from the chicken and place on the top rack in the oven.

One hour before mealtime, remove the plastic wrap from the potatoes and place on the lower rack in the oven.

Thirty minutes before mealtime, brush the remaining butter over the chicken and stir the potatoes.

Fifteen minutes before mealtime, remove the chicken from the oven and poke a fork into the thigh to make sure the juices are not pink. If the juices run clear, cover with aluminum foil and let stand for 10 minutes. If they are pink, return it to the oven for 10 more minutes, or until the juices run clear.

Ten minutes before mealtime, place the saucepan over medium heat, bring to a boil, and cook for 5 minutes, or until tender. (Alternatively, cook the asparagus in the microwave on high heat for 5 minutes, or until tender.) Drain off the water.

Place the whole chicken in the center of a serving plate and arrange the potatoes and asparagus around the chicken.

SALMON WITH HERBED CHEESE AND BROCCOLI

J: I know you are probably thinking, "Me make fish . . . how about No." I
promise you this dish is perfect date food, not only tasty but easy and
impressive. Come on, three ingredients including the side dish. It doesn't
get any easier than that. All the seasoning comes from the cheese, so
it's foolproof and only takes about 5 minutes to get ready. Better yet,
it cooks in foil so there are no pans to wash.

SERVES 2

2 (6-ounce) salmon fillets

2 tablespoons herbed cheese
spread, such as Alouette or
Rondelé

2 cups broccoli florets

 FOOD FOR THOUGHT

Salmon is rich in minerals and
vitamins A, D, E, B6, and B12.
But most important it contains
omega-3 oil, which is linked
to decreasing the risk of heart
disease, certain cancers, and
even depression. So not only
are you making a delicious
meal, you are helping to keep
your date healthy.

Up to 4 hours before mealtime, place two 12-inch pieces of foil
on a flat work surface. Place a salmon fillet in the center of each
piece of foil and spread one tablespoon of the cheese over each
piece of salmon. Pull two opposite long edges of the foil together
and fold them over a couple of times to seal the foil and form a
loose pouch. Roll the sides of the foil up a couple of times and
press firmly to seal well. Refrigerate until ready to cook.

Place the broccoli in a saucepan and add about 1/2 inch of
water. (Alternatively, if you have a microwave, place the broccoli in a microwave-safe bowl and add a little water. Cover with
plastic wrap or waxed paper.) Refrigerate until ready to cook.

About 30 minutes before mealtime, preheat the oven
to 350°F.

Twenty minutes before mealtime, place the salmon pouches
on the center rack in the oven and bake for 15 minutes, or
until it is no longer translucent. Remove from the oven and let
stand for 5 minutes before unwrapping.

Place the saucepan over
medium heat, bring to a boil,
and cook for 5 minutes, or
until tender. (Alternatively,
cook the broccoli in the
microwave on high heat for
5 minutes, or until tender.)
Carefully drain the water
from the broccoli.

Remove the salmon from
the pouches and place a piece
on one side of each plate.
Arrange the broccoli alongside the salmon and serve
immediately.

SMOKED SALMON ASPARAGUS "RISOTTO"

M: Yes, we know that real risotto uses arborio rice, but we also know that it has to be stirred constantly for 40 minutes and that's not a good way to impress your date. Arborio rice releases more starch as it cooks than other types of rice, making risotto very creamy. This version is still really creamy, but can be prepped ahead of time and finished in less than 15 minutes.

SERVES 2

2¼ cups water

3 teaspoons dried chicken bouillon

1 cup white rice

½ pound asparagus

4 ounces smoked salmon

1 cup heavy cream

½ cup grated Parmesan cheese

Salt and pepper

 FOOD TRIVIA

Here's a little more asparagus trivia. In Roman times, asparagus was simply and quickly prepared by boiling the shoots. The Emperor Augustus is supposed to have been rather fond of it and to have originated a saying, "Quicker than you can cook asparagus." Personally, I'm just grateful that saying didn't last.

Up to 4 hours before mealtime, place the water and chicken bouillon in a saucepan and bring to a boil. Stir in the rice, cover, and cook over medium-low heat for 20 minutes, or until the liquid is absorbed. Transfer the rice to a large sauté pan, cover, and refrigerate until ready to cook.

Remove and discard the ends from the asparagus and cut the remainder into 1-inch pieces. Place the asparagus in a saucepan and add about ½ inch of water. Bring to a boil, and cook over medium heat for 5 minutes, or until tender. (Alternatively, if you have a microwave, place in a microwave-safe bowl and add a little water. Cover with waxed paper or plastic wrap and microwave on high for 3 minutes, or until tender.) Drain the water and refrigerate until ready to use.

Cut the smoked salmon into ¼-inch-thick strips, cover, and refrigerate until ready to use.

Fifteen minutes before mealtime, remove the pan with the rice from the refrigerator, uncover, and transfer to the stove. Add the cream and cook over medium-high heat, stirring frequently, for 5 minutes, or until it just begins to boil. Add the Parmesan cheese and cook over medium heat, stirring constantly, for 5 minutes, or until it just begins to thicken. Stir in the asparagus, season with salt and pepper, and cook for 2 minutes to heat through. Stir in the salmon and remove from the heat.

Spoon some of the risotto onto each plate and serve immediately.

CRAB CAKES WITH ROASTED RED PEPPER SAUCE

J: This recipe seems complicated, but it's truly not hard to do, there are just a few steps. The good news is all the work (and mess) can be done well ahead of time. I know lump crabmeat is expensive, but don't be tempted to use anything else. It's still cheaper than going out to eat and your date wouldn't be impressed by mushy crab cakes. If you are lucky enough to have a seafood store near you that carries fresh lump crab, by all means, get it fresh. Otherwise, the canned lump crab is a fine substitute.

SERVES 2

ROASTED RED PEPPER SAUCE

2 red peppers

1 clove garlic

1 cup mayonnaise

Salt and pepper

VINAIGRETTE

1 tablespoon lime juice

2 tablespoons canola oil

CRAB CAKES

1 jalapeño pepper

2 tablespoons chopped chives

1 tablespoon lime juice

1 cup breadcrumbs

1 pound lump crabmeat

2 tablespoons canola oil

SALAD

3 cups salad greens

To make the sauce: *Up to 1 day before mealtime,* roast the red peppers by placing each whole pepper directly on the gas stove burner (if you have an electric stove do this under the broiler) and cook, turning occasionally, for 10 to 15 minutes, until they are almost completely black. Place them in a bowl, cover tightly with plastic wrap, and let stand for 10 minutes. (The steam will make the skin peel right off.) Scrape the blackened skin off the peppers and discard, cut the peppers in half, and remove and discard the stems and seeds.

Dice half of one of the peppers into 1/4-inch pieces and set aside. Place the remaining peppers in a blender. Peel the garlic, roughly chop, and add to the blender with the mayonnaise. Purée for 30 seconds, or until smooth, and season with salt and pepper.

To make the vinaigrette: Place 2 tablespoons of the sauce in a small bowl. Add the lime juice and the oil and stir vigorously with a whisk or fork. Season with salt and pepper, cover with plastic wrap, and refrigerate until ready to use.

To make the crab cakes: Cut the jalapeño in half and remove and discard the stem and seeds. Finely chop the jalapeño and place in a large bowl. Add the chives, lime juice, diced red peppers, and 1/3 cup of the red pepper sauce to the bowl and stir well. Add the breadcrumbs and crabmeat and stir until just combined, being careful not to break up the crabmeat too much. Form the crabmeat mixture into 4 patties and place on a plate. Cover with plastic wrap and refrigerate until ready to cook.

Place the remaining red pepper sauce in a small bowl, cover with plastic wrap, and refrigerate until ready to use.

Fifteen minutes before mealtime, heat the canola oil in a large sauté pan. Add the crab cakes and cook for 5 to 6 minutes on each side, until golden brown.

Meanwhile, assemble the salad. Place the salad greens in a bowl, stir the vinaigrette well, and pour over the greens. Toss until well coated.

Arrange half of the greens on one side of each plate. Place 1 or 2 crab cakes next to the salad, spoon some of the sauce on top, and serve immediately.

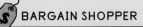

SHRIMP IN COCONUT MILK

J: This is another recipe I tried in France. It actually comes from the French colony of Martinique, an island in the Caribbean, which explains the coconut milk and banana combination. The coconut milk and curry are very mild and give just a hint of the Caribbean flavor. It's scrumptious, easy to make, and a surprising change from your usual date food.

SERVES 2

SHRIMP IN COCONUT MILK

1 tablespoon olive oil

12 ounces peeled and deveined raw shrimp

1 small onion

2 tomatoes

2 cloves garlic

1 teaspoon dried chicken bouillon

1 cup water

1 teaspoon curry powder

Salt and pepper

1/2 cup coconut milk

RICE

1 3/4 cups water

3/4 cup rice

BANANA

1 teaspoon olive oil

2 bananas

To prepare the shrimp: *Up to 3 hours before mealtime,* place the olive oil in a large sauté pan over medium-high heat. Add the shrimp and cook, stirring frequently, for 3 to 4 minutes, until the shrimp begin to turn pink and curl up. Remove the shrimp from the pan, cool slightly, cover, and refrigerate until ready to use.

Peel the onion and dice into 1/4- to 1/2-inch pieces. Cut the tomatoes in quarters, remove and discard the seeds, and cut into 1/4- to 1/2-inch pieces. Peel the garlic and finely chop. Add the onion, tomato, and garlic to the pan and cook over medium-high heat, stirring frequently, for 15 minutes, or until the tomatoes are cooked down to a sauce. Add the chicken bouillon and water and cook for 5 minutes, or until the mixture just begins to boil. Remove from the heat to cool slightly, cover, and refrigerate in the pan until ready to use.

To prepare the rice: *Thirty minutes before mealtime,* bring the water to a boil in a small saucepan and add the rice. Stir well, cover, and cook over low heat for 20 minutes, or until most of the liquid is absorbed. Remove from the heat and let stand for 5 minutes.

To prepare the banana: *Ten minutes before mealtime,* place the olive oil in a small sauté pan over medium-high heat. Peel the bananas and cut in half widthwise and lengthwise. Place the pieces in the pan, and cook for 1 to 2 minutes on each side, or until browned.

Meanwhile, place the sauté pan with the tomato mixture on the stove over medium-high heat and cook for 5 minutes, or until it begins to boil. Add the shrimp and curry powder and cook for 2 minutes, or until heated through. Season with salt and pepper, stir in the coconut milk, and remove from the heat.

Place some of the rice in the center of each plate and top with some of the shrimp mixture. Arrange 4 of the banana pieces around the rice and serve immediately.

STRAWBERRY WHIPPED
TOPPING DESSERT

HAM AND PINEAPPLE
SANDWICHES

GRAPE JELLY
MEATBALLS

SALAMI
TORTILLA
ROLLUPS

SHRIMP
CHEESE
PUFFS

'80s PARTY

Just about everyone we know agrees that the '80s were one of the wackiest times in history. With the tied–on-the-side T-shirts, crimped hair, side ponytails, and guys with gold chains and outrageous chest hair, the '80s were like totally awesome in every way. So why not celebrate good times and experience the '80s yourself? These recipes will put you well on your way to creating a memorable night. In the '80s, food was all about saving time and making it easy, a philosophy we agree with wholeheartedly. And, although they may sound a little scary, we have tried all the recipes and vouch that they are **totally tasteworthy**, despite their '80s qualities. The most frightening part is that our family still makes a lot of these things for family parties.

Along with the recipes, we've included some other pointers on how to have a totally gnarly party by including costume contests, trivia, and of course, crazy '80s music. Go as far as you want with it, but we'll tell you from experience, if the host is enthusiastic about the theme, the guests will get into it that much more.

HAM AND PINEAPPLE SANDWICHES

M: My mom thinks these might be more '60s than '80s, but they sound '80s to me, so here they are. These open-faced grilled cheese sandwiches are easy to make and sure to get a comment or two from your friends.

MAKES 24 PIECES

6 slices white bread

6 slices ham

6 pineapple rings

6 slices Swiss cheese

Preheat the broiler to high.

Place the bread on a baking sheet and place under the broiler for 2 to 3 minutes on each side, or until lightly browned. (This can also be done in a toaster.) Place a piece of ham on each piece of bread and top with a pineapple ring and a piece of cheese. Place the pan under the broiler and cook for 5 minutes, or until the cheese is melted and begins to brown. (Watch them carefully because they can go from brown to black quickly.) Remove the pan from the broiler, cut each sandwich diagonally into 4 pieces, and place on a serving platter.

GRAPE JELLY MEATBALLS

M: Okay, don't freak out when you see the ingredients on this one. Yes, grape jelly in the sauce. Trust me, they're delicious. This is one of the recipes that my family still makes all the time and everyone loves them.

MAKES ABOUT
60 MEATBALLS

1 small onion

1 1/2 pounds ground beef

1 cup breadcrumbs

2 eggs

1 teaspoon salt

1 (18-ounce) jar grape jelly

1 (12-ounce) bottle chili sauce

Preheat the oven to 350°F.

Peel and finely chop the onion. Place the ground beef, onion, breadcrumbs, eggs, and salt in a large bowl and mix with your hands until thoroughly combined. Roll the mixture into 1-inch balls and place them on a baking sheet. Bake for 30 to 35 minutes, until cooked through. Remove the meatballs from the pan and place on paper towels to drain.

Place the grape jelly and chili sauce in a microwave-safe serving container and stir until combined. Place the meatballs in the sauce and stir until completely coated. (The meatballs can be refrigerated for several days and reheated on the stovetop or in the microwave for about 10 minutes, stirring occasionally to ensure they are heated through.) Serve with toothpicks on the side.

SHRIMP CHEESE PUFFS

M: Shrimp is something that I don't often serve at parties simply because it costs too much. But, this recipe uses the tiny little shrimp that are usually pretty cheap. Use frozen shrimp: the canned ones taste too fishy, or if you don't like shrimp, you can leave them out.

MAKES 28 PUFFS

1/2 cup butter, softened

1/2 pound shredded cheddar cheese

1 egg

7 slices white bread

28 cooked shrimp

> ### DRESSING THE PART
>
> A costume contest is a fun way to get people into the theme. You can give them a few ideas ahead of time if you want. For the girls: leggings and leg warmers, side pony tails, crimped hair, big hair scrunchies, big plastic bright colored earrings and bracelets, long T-shirts tied on the side, and anything in fuchsia or bright teal. For the guys: silky shirts, chest hair (fun fur?), gold chains, tapered tight pants, head and wrist bands, the *Miami Vice* look, and polyester jogging suits.

Preheat the oven to 350°F.

Stir together the butter and cheese in a large bowl. Separate the egg white from the yolk. Place the white in a separate bowl and stir the yolk into the cheese mixture. Beat the egg white with a whisk or fork for 2 to 3 minutes, until the egg white forms peaks that remain upright when the whisk is pulled out. Spoon the egg white into the cheese mixture and gently fold it in by running a rubber spatula or spoon down the edge to the bottom of the bowl, bringing it up the other side, and folding the cheese over the egg white. Continue this process until it is fairly well mixed. (It is better to have a few streaks of egg white than to overmix and deflate the whites and keep them from puffing up.)

Remove and discard the crusts from the bread (or reserve for another purpose), cut each slice into quarters, and place the pieces on a baking sheet. Place 1 shrimp on each piece of bread and top with a rounded teaspoon of the cheese mixture. Bake for 15 to 18 minutes, until golden brown. Place on a serving platter, and serve immediately.

SALAMI TORTILLA ROLLUPS

M: I used to eat these all the time as an after-school snack. Who knew I was actually paying homage to another generation? Make them with or without the pickles; it doesn't matter.

MAKES ABOUT
36 PIECES

4 10-inch flour tortillas

6 ounces cream cheese

1/2 pound thinly sliced hard salami

8 dill pickle spears

Lay a tortilla on a flat work surface and spread one quarter of the cream cheese over the entire tortilla. Arrange one quarter of the salami over the cream cheese, covering as much of it as possible. Lay 2 pickle spears end to end on one side of the tortilla and tightly roll the tortilla around the pickle. Roll the tortilla in plastic wrap and repeat with the remaining ingredients. Refrigerate the rolls for at least 30 minutes. Cut about 1 inch off of each end of the rolls and discard. Remove the plastic wrap, cut the rolls into 1/2-inch-thick pieces, and place on a serving platter.

 PARTY STARTERS

How about a slogan contest? Have your friends try to figure out what product was using these slogans in the '80s. Whoever gets the most right wins a prize.

Where's the Beef? (Beef Commission)

Reach out and touch someone. (Bell Telephone)

I want hot stuff! (Chef Boyardee)

You can smile, America. (Chuck E. Cheese)

Avoid the Noid. (Dominos Pizza)

Just for the taste of it! (Diet Coke)

Show 'em you're a tiger. (Frosted Flakes)

We bring good things to life. (G.E.)

The Great American Chocolate Bar! (Hershey's)

Great taste to go! (Hostess Snack Cakes)

The taste is gonna move you! (Juicy Fruit Gum)

We do chicken right! (Kentucky Fried Chicken)

The brand that fits. (Lee Jeans)

Mikey likes it. (Life Cereal)

Good time . . . great taste. (McDonald's)

It's a creamy licking chocolate sensation. (Oreo Cookies)

Two scoops. (Raisin Bran)

Of course, if you are going to have contests then you have to have prizes. How about giving the winners things that were introduced in the '80s? You can usually find old movies pretty cheap. How about *Ferris Bueller's Day Off*, *The Breakfast Club*, or *Weird Science*? Otherwise, food always works. Pop Secret Pop Corn, Fruit Roll Ups, Snapple, and Hershey's Kisses with Almonds were all introduced in the '80s.

STRAWBERRY WHIPPED TOPPING DESSERT

M: Is it a cake? Is it a Jell-O mold? We may never know. But we do know it's a delightfully light strawberry shortcake dessert that is super easy to make and tastes good, too.

SERVES 12

1 (6-ounce) box strawberry gelatin

1 cup boiling water

30 ounces frozen straw-berries, thawed

16 ounces whipped topping

1 (1-pound) prepared angel food cake

Place the gelatin in a large bowl, add the boiling water, and stir for 2 minutes, or until completely dissolved. Cut the strawberries in quarters and add to the gelatin. Add the whipped topping and stir until combined. Tear the angel food cake into 1- to 2-inch pieces and place half of them in the bottom of a 9 by 13-inch baking pan. Spread half of the strawberry mixture over the cake and repeat with a second layer of cake and strawberries. Refrigerate for at least 2 hours before serving. Cut into squares and place on small serving plates.

♫♪ MUSIC

Music is another important part of the party. Put together some CDs with popular '80s music. You could also do a lip-synch contest. Put all the music for the contest on one CD and pass around a list of titles for people to choose from. Make sure you have some silly stuff on the list to get the crowd going. I can still see some of my friends camp-ing it up to Dolly Parton's "9 to 5," The Bangles' "Walk Like an Egyptian," and Kenny Log-gins' "Footloose" (although my furniture didn't handle that one so well).

SATISFYING YOUR SWEET TOOTH

Everyone loves desserts, but not everyone wants to spend a lot of time making them. Being the accommodating people that we are, we included a **variety of recipes** here. There are bars, which are super fast to put together and make a lot. There are cookies, which are also easy, but take a little longer to bake them all. And there are a few fancier desserts for special occasions or to go with the "Impressing Your Date" dinners. None of these recipes are difficult, some just have more steps than others. Just choose the recipe that suits your mood.

BROWNIE BITES

M: My grandmother used to make these easy cookies for us all the time (see photo on opposite page). They are chocolaty, chewy little bites that taste a lot like brownies. (That would probably be why they are called brownie bites.) You may want to think about making a double batch, because they seem to disappear quickly.

MAKES ABOUT
4 DOZEN COOKIES

12 ounces chocolate chips

1/4 cup butter

1 (14-ounce) can sweetened condensed milk

1 teaspoon vanilla

1 cup flour

1 cup chopped walnuts

Preheat the oven to 350°F.

Place the chocolate chips and butter in a small saucepan and cook over low heat, stirring constantly, for 5 to 7 minutes, until all of the chips are melted. (Alternatively, if you have a microwave, place the chocolate chips and butter in a large microwave-safe bowl and microwave on high heat for 1 minute, then stir. If the chocolate is not all melted, place it back in the microwave for 15 seconds at a time, stirring after each time, until it is completely melted.)

Add the sweetened condensed milk, vanilla, flour, and walnuts and stir until combined.

Drop teaspoonfuls of the dough 2 inches apart on a baking sheet and bake for 10 minutes, or until the tops look dry. Let cool on the baking sheet for 2 minutes, then cool on parchment or waxed paper.

POTATO CHIP COOKIES

J: Okay, so I know you're thinking, "Potato chips in cookies, that's too weird." But I promise you these are a real treat. The potato chips give the cookies a little extra crunch and a nice salty flavor. Besides, what else are you going to do with all the little chips in the bottom of the bag?

MAKES ABOUT
4 DOZEN COOKIES

1 cup butter, softened

1/2 cup sugar

3/4 cup crushed ridged potato chips

1/2 cup chopped pecans

1 teaspoon vanilla

2 cups flour

Confectioners' sugar for dusting (optional)

Preheat the oven to 350°F.

Place the butter and sugar in a large bowl and stir until smooth. Add the potato chips, pecans, and vanilla and stir until combined. Add the flour and stir until incorporated. Drop teaspoonfuls of the dough about 2 inches apart on a baking sheet and bake for 12 to 15 minutes, until the edges are lightly browned. Cool on parchment or waxed paper and sprinkle with confectioners' sugar, if desired.

> ### 🏅 FOOD TRIVIA
>
> The world's largest potato chip was produced in 1990 by Pringles Company, in Jackson, Tennessee. It measured 25 inches by 14 inches. That gives a whole new meaning to, "I'm only going to eat a couple of chips."

*Potato Chip Cookies
and Brownie Bites
(recipe on opposite page)*

PEANUT BUTTER CUP BARS

M: These bars are so good that you will have to hide them from your
friends if you want them to last more than 5 minutes. They are super
easy to make. In fact, the hardest part about these melt-in-your-
mouth bars is waiting for them to cool enough to eat.

MAKES 48 BARS

1 cup butter, softened

1 (18-ounce) jar peanut
butter (about 2 cups)

1½ cups graham cracker
crumbs (about 12 squares)

3 cups confectioners' sugar

12 ounces chocolate chips

Preheat the oven to 350°F.

Place the butter and peanut butter in a large bowl and stir
until smooth. Add the graham cracker crumbs and sugar and
stir until completely combined. Spread the mixture in a 9 by
13-inch baking pan and bake for 30 minutes. Remove from
the oven and let stand for 5 minutes to cool slightly. Sprinkle
the warm bars with the chips, let stand for 2 minutes until the
chips begin to melt, and then spread them evenly over the top.
Cool slightly and cut into 48 squares while the chocolate is
still warm.

 FOOD TRIVIA

Here is a little trivia from our
friends at Hershey's. (Hey,
we like anyone that makes
chocolate.) Reese's Peanut
Butter Cups are Hershey's
biggest seller, but in the
1950s, the company tried a
chocolate marshmallow cup
that showed real promise.
Unfortunately, the product
had to be discontinued—the
marshmallow filling had a
tendency to explode when
shipped over the high altitude
of the Rocky Mountains.
Imagine what a mess that
would be.

*Peanut Butter Cup Bars
and Pecan Pie Bars
(recipe on opposite page)*

PECAN PIE BARS

M: I know that bars may sound old-fashioned, but they're just like cookies and they're a lot faster to make. These bars are like pecan pie with a thicker crust and less filling so you can eat them with your hands (see photo on opposite page). If you are making these for a special occasion, it looks cool if you use pecan halves instead of chopped pecans and arrange them in rows on top of the filling.

MAKES 48 BARS

CRUST

1 cup brown sugar

2 cups flour

1 cup butter, melted

FILLING

4 eggs

2 cups chopped pecans

1/4 cup flour

1 teaspoon salt

3 cups brown sugar

1 teaspoon vanilla

Preheat the oven to 350°F.

To prepare the crust: Place the brown sugar and flour in a 9 by 13-inch pan and stir until combined. Add the butter and stir until evenly moistened. Pat the crust into the bottom of the pan and bake for 15 minutes. Remove the pan from the oven and lower the temperature to 325°F.

To prepare the filling: Place the eggs in a large bowl and beat until the whites are broken up and completely incorporated into the yolks. Add the pecans, flour, salt, brown sugar, and vanilla and mix until combined. Spread the mixture evenly over the crust and bake for 40 minutes, or until the filling is firm. Cool completely and cut into 48 squares.

 **BARGAIN SHOPPER**

The first time I bought butter, I couldn't believe it was almost $5 a pound. As much as I like to bake, that doesn't work for me. I consulted my favorite bargain shopper (Mom) and she said that she usually buys it at a warehouse store where it costs less than $2 a pound or she buys it when it's on sale at the grocery store. Either way, she buys a lot at a time and puts it in the freezer, where it will keep for several months.

CRÊPES WITH ICE CREAM AND CHOCOLATE SAUCE

J: While I was studying in France, my friend Lindsay insisted I try this little crêpe place she had found. It turned out to be down a sketchy alley and I began wondering what we were doing there until I went in. The shop was filled with a number of incredibly tasty-looking items, but I decided to order these and it was all over. They were so yummy that I had to order them every time we went there (which was more often than I'd like to admit). Crêpes are easy to make, and any extras can be refrigerated for several days or frozen for up to a month.

SERVES 4

4 eggs

1 1/2 cups milk

2 tablespoons canola oil

1 cup flour

1/2 teaspoon salt

2/3 cup chocolate chips

1/2 cup heavy cream

1/4 cup sugar

1 pint vanilla ice cream

 FOOD FOR THOUGHT

Okay, admittedly there is nothing low-cal about this recipe, but all is not lost. Crêpes are only about 95 calories each. So if you skip the chocolate sauce and go for fresh strawberries, you could save a lot of calories and still have a luscious dessert.

Place the eggs in a blender and pulse a few times to break them up. Add the milk, oil, flour, and salt and blend until smooth.

Heat a small (8- or 9-inch) nonstick sauté pan over medium-high heat. Place a small amount of oil on a paper towel and rub it over the surface of the pan. Pour in 1/4 cup of the crêpe batter and quickly swirl the pan around until it covers the entire bottom of the pan. Cook for 2 minutes, or until the crêpe is set in the center. Loosen the edges with a spatula and turn the crêpe over. Cook for 1 minute, or until very lightly browned, and remove from the pan. Repeat the process with the remaining batter, oiling the pan before cooking each crêpe.

Place the chocolate chips, cream, and sugar in a small saucepan and cook over low heat, stirring frequently, for 5 minutes, or until the chocolate is melted and the sugar is dissolved. Remove from the heat and serve warm.

Fold the crêpes in quarters and arrange three in the center of each plate. Top with a scoop of vanilla ice cream and spoon the chocolate sauce on top.

LEMON SUGAR COOKIES

J: I am generally not a huge fan of lemon desserts, but these cookies are so crisp and delicate that they melt in your mouth. The bonus is that they are incredibly fast and easy to make. In 30 minutes you can go from sitting on the couch thinking about cookies to actually eating them, and that's never a bad thing.

MAKES ABOUT
4 DOZEN COOKIES

1 cup butter, softened

1 cup sugar plus extra for dipping

1 lemon

1 egg

1/2 teaspoon lemon extract

2 cups flour

1/2 teaspoon baking powder

 FOOD FOR THOUGHT

I have a major sweet tooth and I get irritated when I want something sweet but feel like I shouldn't indulge. If you're like me, these cookies are the answer. Even though they are sweet and buttery, they are only about 70 calories per cookie so you can indulge without feeling guilty.

Preheat the oven to 375°F.

Place the butter and sugar in a large bowl and stir until combined. Remove the zest from the lemon by running it over the smallest openings on a grater. (Be careful not to grate the bitter white part of the lemon peel, known as the "pith.") Add the egg, lemon zest, and lemon extract to the bowl and stir well. Add the flour and baking powder and mix until completely incorporated.

Place some sugar in a small bowl. Drop rounded teaspoonfuls of the dough about 3 inches apart on a baking sheet. Dip the bottom of a glass into the dough to make it sticky and then dip it into the sugar. Press down lightly on each cookie with the bottom of the glass to flatten them, dipping the glass in the sugar for each cookie.

Bake for 10 to 12 minutes, until the edges of the cookies just begin to brown. Cool on parchment or waxed paper.

LAZY PINWHEEL COOKIES

J: I love pinwheel cookies . . . when someone else makes them. Making real pinwheel cookies is too much like work, so I did what I do best—I made it easier. I put the chocolate on one side and the vanilla on the other (see photo on opposite page). If you want to roll out both doughs, layer them, and roll them up, go ahead. But for me, the lazy way works just fine.

MAKES ABOUT
5 DOZEN
COOKIES

3/4 cup butter, softened

1 cup sugar

2 eggs

1 teaspoon vanilla

2 1/2 cups flour

1 teaspoon baking powder

1/2 teaspoon salt

1/2 cup chocolate chips

Place the butter and sugar in a large bowl and stir until smooth. Add the eggs and vanilla and stir well. Add the flour, baking powder, and salt and stir until completely incorporated.

Place a 2-foot-long piece of plastic wrap on a flat surface. Spread half of the dough down the center of the plastic to form an 18-inch-long, 2-inch-wide rectangle. Set the other half of the dough aside.

Place the chocolate chips in a small saucepan and cook over low heat, stirring constantly, for 3 to 4 minutes, until the chocolate is melted. (Alternatively, if you have a microwave, place the chocolate chips in a small microwave-safe bowl and microwave on high heat for 30 seconds, then stir. If the chocolate is not all melted, place it back in the microwave for 15 seconds at a time, stirring after each time, until it is completely melted.)

Stir the melted chocolate into the remaining dough and spread evenly over the white dough. Fold the excess plastic wrap over the dough and smooth with your hands to form a 1 1/2- to 2-inch-diameter log. Lift up the excess plastic wrap and use it to roll the log to one edge of the wrap. Tightly wrap the log in the plastic wrap and refrigerate for 30 minutes.

Preheat the oven to 400°F.

Remove the plastic wrap from the roll and cut into 1/4-inch-thick slices. Arrange the slices on a baking sheet about 2 inches apart and bake for 10 to 12 minutes, until lightly browned. Cool on parchment or waxed paper.

ANYTHING GOES COOKIES

J: You can pretty much use any dried fruit, nuts, or chips that you like in these cookies. Just follow the basic recipe and change the last four ingredients to suit your tastes. You can stay mainstream with them or go crazy and add something out of the ordinary, like dried tropical fruits and macadamia nuts.

MAKES ABOUT
4 DOZEN COOKIES

1 cup butter, softened

1 cup firmly packed brown sugar

1/2 cup granulated sugar

2 eggs

1 teaspoon vanilla

2 cups flour

1 teaspoon baking soda

1/2 teaspoon salt

2 cups oatmeal

1 cup raisins

1 cup coconut

1 cup chopped walnuts

1 cup white chocolate chips

Preheat the oven to 350°F.

Place the butter, brown sugar, and granulated sugar in a large bowl and stir until completely smooth. Add the eggs and vanilla and stir until combined. Add the flour, baking soda, salt, and oatmeal and stir until the flour is completely incorporated. Fold in the raisins, coconut, walnuts, and white chocolate chips.

Drop golf ball–size spoonfuls of the dough onto a baking sheet about 3 inches apart and bake for 15 to 17 minutes, until lightly browned on the edges and set in the center. Let the cookies sit on the baking sheet for 2 minutes and cool on parchment or waxed paper.

Anything Goes Cookies and Lazy Pinwheel Cookies (recipe on opposite page)

PUMPKIN CAKE WITH CREAM CHEESE FROSTING

M: I love pumpkin in just about any form, but put it in a cake with cream cheese frosting, and there's no holding me back. This cake is perfect to bring to a hang-out night with your friends or for you and your roomies to munch on for dessert. Or breakfast! Hey, pumpkin is a fruit and cake has grain and dairy products . . . sounds like breakfast to me.

MAKES ONE
9 BY 13-INCH
CAKE

PUMPKIN CAKE

1/2 cup butter, softened

1 cup sugar

1 cup firmly packed brown sugar

1 (15-ounce) can pumpkin

2 teaspoons vanilla

3 eggs

2 teaspoons baking soda

1/4 teaspoon salt

2 1/2 teaspoons pumpkin pie spice

2 1/3 cups flour

CREAM CHEESE FROSTING

8 ounces cream cheese, softened

2 tablespoons butter, softened

3 cups confectioners' sugar

2 tablespoons milk

1 teaspoon vanilla

To prepare the cake: Preheat the oven to 350°F. Lightly coat a 9 by 13-inch baking pan with butter or cooking spray.

Place the butter, sugar, and brown sugar in a large bowl and stir until completely smooth. Add the pumpkin and vanilla and stir well. Add the eggs one at a time, stirring after each addition until completely incorporated. Add the baking soda, salt, and pumpkin pie spice and stir until combined. Add the flour and stir until incorporated. Pour the batter into the baking pan and bake for 35 to 40 minutes, until the cake springs back when pressed gently in the center. Cool completely.

To prepare the frosting: Place the cream cheese and butter in a large bowl and stir until completely smooth. Add the confectioners' sugar, milk, and vanilla and stir until smooth. Spread the frosting over the cooled cake.

APPLE PASTIES

J: When I was an exchange student in France, I was only an hour and a half from London, so of course, I had to make several trips there. On one trip while wandering around Covent Garden watching the street performers, I came across a vendor selling pasties. I had wanted to try this traditional English dish and when I saw one with apples I knew it was time. Oh man, was it good. In fact, it might be the best apple dessert I've ever had, and coming from me, an apple-dessert connoisseur, that's saying a lot.

1 egg

1/2 cup sour cream

1/3 cup sugar

1 tablespoon flour

1/4 teaspoon salt

1/2 teaspoon cinnamon

3 apples

2 prepared piecrusts

Preheat the oven to 375°F.

Separate the egg, placing the egg yolk in a large bowl, reserving the egg white for later use. Add the sour cream, sugar, flour, salt, and cinnamon and stir until combined. Peel and core the apples and dice into 1/2-inch pieces. Add the apples to the bowl and stir until completely coated.

Lay the piecrusts on a flat work surface and spoon one-half of the apple mixture in the center of each piecrust, avoiding the edges. Fold the dough over to form a half circle, gently roll up about 3/4 inch of the open edges and press gently to seal. Lightly beat the egg white until broken up, but not frothy. and brush on the dough. Bake for 30 to 35 minutes, until golden brown. Cut each pasty in half and serve warm.

🏅 FOOD TRIVIA

Pasties are a traditional English dish that were first mentioned in writings from the twelfth century. Pasties became a staple of Cornish miners because they were a meal unto themselves, containing meat, potatoes, and sometimes even apples at one end for dessert. Also, because the tin mines contained arsenic, pasties were a way for miners to eat without contaminating their food. They could hold the pasty by the thick crust edge, eat the main part without touching it with their hands, and throw the crust edge away to avoid arsenic poisoning. Good call.

MINI BLUEBERRY TURNOVERS

M: When we were testing the recipes for this book, all of our neighbors and friends thought we needed to try this one again. Not because it needed work, they just wanted more. Blueberry Turnovers are super easy to make and absolutely delicious. They would make a perfect ending to an "Impressing Your Date" meal. Serve them warm and believe me, your date will be impressed.

MAKES 9 MINI TURNOVERS

4 ounces cream cheese, softened

1 egg

1/4 cup sugar plus extra for sprinkling

1 sheet puff pastry, thawed

1/2 pint blueberries (1 cup)

Preheat the oven to 400°F. Lightly coat a baking sheet with oil or cooking spray.

Place the cream cheese in a small bowl and stir until completely smooth. Separate the egg yolk from the egg white. Place the egg white in a small bowl and add the egg yolk to the cream cheese. Add the sugar to the cream cheese and stir until combined.

Lay the sheet of puff pastry on a flat surface and cut into 9 small squares. Spoon a tablespoon of the cream cheese mixture down the center of each square from one corner to the opposite corner. Press the blueberries into the cream cheese. Fold the sides into the center, wet the points with a little water, and press tightly to seal. (Press the sides tightly together or they will open while they bake.)

Place the turnovers on the baking pan, brush with the egg white, and sprinkle lightly with sugar. (If you are making these ahead, you can cover the pan with plastic wrap and refrigerate them for up to 4 hours before baking.)

Bake for 15 to 17 minutes, until golden brown. Remove from the oven and serve warm.

CHOCOLATE PEAR TART

M: This is a standard tart in France, and I thought the combination of pears and chocolate on flaky pastry was so tasty I had to bring it back. This would be a perfect ending to one of the "Impressing Your Date" meals. It's easy, tastes great, looks really cool, and can all be done ahead of time.

SERVES 6

1 sheet puff pastry, thawed

2 tablespoons sugar

1/4 cup chocolate chips

2 tablespoons heavy cream

1 (15-ounce) can pear halves

FOOD FOR THOUGHT

One medium pear can contain as much as 5 grams of fiber, which is beneficial to your heart, digestive system, and cholesterol levels. The same size pear contains only 100 calories even though it contains high concentrations of levulose, which is the sweetest of the natural sugars. Sweet, juicy, and healthy, how can you pass that up?

Preheat the oven to 400°F. Lightly coat a baking sheet with oil or cooking spray.

Place the sheet of puff pastry on the baking sheet and bake for 12 to 15 minutes, until golden brown. Remove from the oven and cool completely. (Turn the oven off; the rest of the tart does not require baking.)

Meanwhile, place the sugar, chocolate chips, and cream in a small saucepan. Cook over medium-low heat, stirring constantly, for 5 minutes, or until the chocolate is completely melted. Remove from the heat and cool to room temperature.

Drain the pear halves and cut each one into 8 wedges. Place the wedges on paper towels and let drain for at least 15 minutes. (If the pears have too much juice on them it will make the chocolate watery.)

Spread the chocolate over the top of the puff pastry, avoiding about 1 inch around the outside edge. Shingle the pear wedges over the chocolate. (The tart can be kept at room temperature for several hours before serving, but leftovers should be covered with plastic wrap and refrigerated.)

INDEX